Choices Matter – Everyday!

Choices Matter – Everyday!

How to Get the Most Out of Your Choices and Your Life

Barry Gallagher

Copyright © 2025, Barry Gallagher

All rights reserved. Printed in the U.S.A.

No part of this publication may be reproduced or transmitted in any form or by any means, electronic or mechanical, including photocopy, recording or any information storage and retrieval system now known or to be invented, without permission in writing from the publisher, except by a reviewer who wishes to quote brief passages in connection with a review written for inclusion in a magazine, newspaper or broadcast.

Quantity Purchases:
Companies, professional groups, clubs, and other organizations may qualify for special terms when ordering quantities of this title. For information, email info@ebooks2go.net,
or call (847) 598-1150 ext. 4141.
www.ebooks2go.net

Published in the United States by eBooks2go, Inc.
1827 Walden Office Square, Suite 260, Schaumburg, IL 60173

ISBN: 978-1-5457-6361-2

Library of Congress Cataloging in Publication

TABLE OF CONTENTS

Chapter One Choose to Choose 1

Chapter Two Choose to Manage Your Mind 21

Chapter Three Choose to Set Goals 43

Chapter Four Choose Your Words—Carefully 71

Chapter Five Choose to Make Your Time Count 95

Chapter Six Choose to Plan 119

Chapter Seven Choose Action 137

Bibliography 163

Acknowledgements 165

About the Author 167

INTRODUCTION

Your life is a result of the choices you make.
If you don't like your life,
it is time to start making better choices.
— **Author Unknown**

This book is based upon the premise that our choices drive our personal success, our wealth, our relationships, our health—everything. After breathing, there is nothing that you will do more in your life than make choices. Unless you want others to run your life, the best life that you can live is a life of choice. Life really is the sum of all our choices. The little ones, the big ones—day after day, they all add up. I believe that we should always do our best to make the right choices. Of course, nobody makes the right choices all the time which means we usually have plenty of opportunities to learn from the wrong ones.

Your life will be much better if you make more good choices than bad ones. As the introductory quote states, if you don't like your life, you have the opportunity to make different choices that could put you in a better place. There is nothing more important to your success than your choices. Every idea in this book is dedicated to helping you make more good choices and fewer bad ones.

Learning to consistently make seven choices can change your life for the best and forever! This book will teach you how to get the most out of your choices, your God given talents, and your life. Believe me, it is a life-changing book that will put you in position to live your best life—a life of choice!

DEDICATION

This book is dedicated to the memory of a man named Robert J. Etienne. Bob Etienne was my step-father from 1954 until his death in 1969. He was a big part of my life for many years. We had a lot in common since we shared the same birthday. Bob also served in the United States Army for a few years and I joined and served for thirty years after he died.

We shared two other things that are also very special in my life. First, he bought a house in 1961 that was located on a beautiful private lake near Rochester, Michigan. Bob loved living on Cranberry Lake and so did the rest of our family. It was an amazing place to spend my teenage years. The second special thing that we shared was a love of writing. Bob spent a lot of time in advertising and also worked as a technical writer. He wrote a lot of advertisements and training manuals for Army equipment operators. Thanks to an encouraging high school English teacher, I developed a great appreciation for the written word. Over the years, I aspired to become the best writer that I could become. Fortunately, my writing skills improved steadily.

Eventually, I developed enough confidence to write books. Unfortunately, Bob passed before he could achieve his dream of writing a book or see me realize that same goal. Now, I have written eight books and this one is number nine. I know that Bob would be proud of me for following through on my passion for writing.

This book is my way of including him in one of my writing projects. I hope this book helps you get the most out of your choices and your life!

CHAPTER 1

CHOOSE TO CHOOSE

Destiny is not a matter of chance; it is a matter of choice. It is not something to be waited for; but rather something to be achieved.
—**William Jennings Bryan**

Choices, choices, choices, choices, and more choices. I like to describe people as "two-legged, living, breathing choice making machines." Our lives are full of choices. I wonder what the average number of choices is for an American in one day. One hundred, two hundred, three hundred or more? What about a lifetime? A half million, a million, or more? It is absolutely mind boggling to think about the impact that choices have on our lives and the world in general. This chapter takes a closer look at why our choices are so important to living our best life and achieving true wealth and happiness. I am confident that this chapter will cause you to think much differently about your choices and how you can use them to achieve everything that you want in life.

"Choice Power" is my expression for the ability to consistently make good choices. After breathing—there is nothing that you do more in life than make choices. I remember a song called *"Love Makes the World Go Round"* from my youth. I liked the song, but I do not think love makes the world "go round." I think love makes the world a much better place, for sure. What makes the world "go round" is choices. Yes, people make choices every minute, every hour and every day that make the world what it is. It is a process that is repeated billions and billions of times. Yes, the power of choice is a force in our world.

Again, the importance of Choice Power was revealed to us over one-hundred fifty years ago by President Abraham Lincoln. Mr. Lincoln said that "People are about as happy as they make up their minds to be." Yes, Choice Power is the awareness that you have the power—to make up your mind and make your own choices. Lincoln's quote can be restated to express the impact that choices have on every aspect of our lives. Let us look at some examples:

> People are as wealthy as they choose to be.
> People are as poor as they choose to be.
> People are as happy as they choose to be.
> People are as miserable as they choose to be.
> People are as kind as they choose to be.
> People are as mean as they choose to be.

Mr. Lincoln's line of thinking demonstrates the true simplicity of the power of choice. In every situation we face, we always have a choice. Sometimes they are difficult choices and sometimes they are easy ones. Will we react positively or negatively to a rude person? Will we respond to difficulties in a positive or negative way? Will we save our money or spend it?

Will we exceed the speed limit to get somewhere on time or slow down and arrive late? The simple fact is this: we are constantly making choices—all day, every day. It is called life!

Yes, we make a lot of choices in a day, a week, and a month. The ability to make more good ones than bad ones is the key to a successful life. Your life will only be as good as the choices you make, one day at a time.

Your Greatest Power!

What is your greatest power? Have you ever asked yourself this question? I did and that is the primary reason I decided to write this book. I discovered my greatest power after reading a book called *Your Greatest Power* by J. Martin Kohe. His remarkable book started changing lives as soon as it was published in 1953.

It changed mine too when I read it nearly thirty years later. The message of this book is so simple and so sensible that it almost defies description.

My greatest power, and your greatest power, is the power of choice. Does this surprise you? Does this amaze you? Does this seem too simplistic? If you answered "Yes" to all these questions, you responded like most people. There certainly must be other aspects of life that are more important than the power of choice, right?

I thought about this question frequently after reading Kohe's book. I also read and re-read the book before I finally gave in to his line of thinking. As Mr. Kohe said in his book, "You can't fight life."

(Kohe, Page 8) After much though and introspection, I made a choice to accept Kohe's statement that my greatest power was, in fact, the power of choice. From that day forward, I have been using this amazing force to build my best life—one choice and one day at a time.

I was twenty-six years old when I first read Mr. Kohe's remarkable book. At the time, I was teaching junior high school Geography and Physical Education in New Baltimore, Michigan. I had a high school diploma and a college degree, but I had never been taught about the power of choice. Yes, this concept had a tremendous impact on my life. It helped me to improve my attitude, my self-understanding, and my teaching. In fact, it helped me improve everything about my life. By understanding the power of choice, I was able to comprehend the control that I really had over my life and my destiny. I finally came to realize that I had the power to make life happen instead of just letting life happen to me!

Choice Power—the power of destiny is the greatest power that any person can possess. Our choices, every single one of them, drive our personal and professional success in some way. There is no magic in this process, just as there is no magic in farming. Farmers reap what they sow. You reap the life you live by the choices that you make or allow others to make for you.

When you learn to master your greatest power, you will create the best life of all—a life of choice! Yes, the power of choice can be your best friend. It is the primary tool that you can use to have everything that you want in life.

A Closer Look at Choice Power

Choice Power will do more to improve your life than any other concept in this book. This is because our choices affect everything that we do or do not do, every day. The power contained in your choices is revealed when we examine the letters behind the word **CHOICE**. Now, it is time to take an in depth look at the power of this amazing word!

Control

Our choices provide us with the opportunity to exert the maximum control in our life. As I mentioned earlier, we make hundreds of choices every day and thousands every month. By the time we go to our graves, we will make millions of choices. Some will be big and some will be small. Many others will be in the middle.

The ability to make good choices gives you the most control over your life. As Thomas Wilson said, "He that will not command his thoughts will soon lose the command of his actions." Mr. Wilson's powerful truth can be rephrased to emphasize the importance of our choices: a person who does not command his choices will lose control of his actions too!

Honesty

Our choices are the gauge that we can use to measure the degree of honesty that we have in our life. Yes, our choices force us, sooner or later, to be honest with ourselves. If we are happy and content with where we are in life, we can reward ourselves with a pat on the back. We have probably made many good choices and are enjoying the benefits of those choices.

However, if we are not happy about the direction our life has taken, we must be honest with ourselves; our choices probably had a lot to do with the situation that we are in. We have probably made some bad ones in the past and are paying the bill, plus interest, on a charge made long ago. Ultimately, an unhappy life means that you are not happy about your choices. The good news is that Choice Power gives us the opportunity to make new choices at any time!

Opportunity

Choice Power allows us to look for the opportunity that exists in a situation instead of focusing on the obstacles. This habit of thinking can empower us to see the potential in each choice instead of the problems. Mr. M. L. Jacks placed the concept of opportunity in perspective when he said, "The pessimist sees the difficulty in every opportunity; the optimist, the opportunity in every difficulty."

Once again, the influence of our choices can be seen when this great quote is rephrased. Yes, the pessimist chooses to see the difficulty in every opportunity while the optimist chooses to see the opportunity in every difficulty.

Many of the greatest people who have ever lived did not have any special skills or powers except the ability to create opportunity. You will create more wealth and success in hour life when you choose opportunity. It is the surest way to create the best life that you can live—a life of choice.

Independence

Our ability to choose is also a barometer of our level of personal independence. The ability to make our own choices is related to our degree of individuality. If we make our own choices and live the life we choose, then we are free to live our own life. However, if we let other people make our choices for us, then we lose much of our personal power.

As children, we did not make too many of the important choices in our lives—our parents and guardians did. As we grew older, we should have been given the opportunity to make more and more of our own choices.

Hopefully, as an adult, you understand the importance of making your own choices and you accept that awesome responsibility. I have learned that our choices are always under control, either ours or somebody else. The question is: "Who controls your choices?"

Creativity

Our choices provide us with a tremendous source of creativity. People who understand the power of choice know that they can create the kind of life that they choose by making one good choice after another. If you know your goals and objectives, the power of choice can convert your dreams into reality. The power of creativity gives us the opportunity to convert setbacks into solutions and obstacles into opportunities.

We always have a choice to create something better in any situation. Choices do not have to be big to make an impact on our life. Even small choices can make a huge difference in your life. The ability to make our own choices is the foundation of building a successful life. We can create our best life using this great power.

Expectations

Choices are always a reflection of our personal expectations. People who have low expectations for themselves and their lives usually make choices that support this outlook on life. If you do not think that you are going to do much in life, you will make choices that are consistent with this view. However, if you have high expectations and you have confidence in your abilities, you will make choices that display your optimistic view of life. Sadly, too many people are weighted down by the limitations that they place upon themselves. Unfortunately, millions of people fail to make choices that they have the power to achieve.

To summarize, Choice Power can give you greater control over every aspect of your life. It can help you develop more honesty about your abilities and your responsibility for developing more of your potential. This amazing power can also help you become an opportunity finder. The power of choice can also help you become more independent in your daily living. It can energize your creative abilities and help you master everyday challenges. Finally, the power of choice can help you raise your expectations for what is possible in your life. I hope that you learn to use the power of choice to create the absolute best life that you can live!

The Dynamics of Choice Power

Your life will only be as good as your worst choices allow. The plain fact is that no choice stands alone. Our choices are linked and joined together like a great chain that connects our life moments. This chain can unify our choices, dreams, and goals into a powerful force in our life. Unfortunately, it can also anchor us to our failures and attach us permanently to low aims and mediocrity. The strength of our "choice chain" is only as strong as our weakest choices.

A person can make great choices in many areas of his or her life and blow it all with one bad choice. We see this played out every single day in the local and national news. Many young athletes and entertainers struggle to overcome drug or alcohol problems when they seem to have everything going for them. How can this happen? Well, it happens like everything else that we have mentioned so far. Everything starts with a choice. When things start to go bad in someone's life, it can always be traced back to a choice, and then another choice. And so on. Maybe just one bad choice, but that can often set you on a bad course. The sad fact is that not even an Olympic sprint champion can outrun the consequences of a bad choice. Yes, bad choices always catch up with us!

The Critical Importance of Supporting Choices

No choice stands alone. We must understand the importance of what I call supporting choices. Supporting choices are secondary choices that we need to make to turn a big choice into reality. For example, you make a choice to lose weight. You decide on your target weight and that is all there is to it, right? Of course, we know that is not how it works!

Losing weight might be your primary choice, but there are many other choices that you must make to achieve your objective. First, you will have to make some changes in the types of foods you eat and the portions. Secondly, you will probably have to start an exercise program if you want to permanently lose your excess weight. Third, you may have to change the timing of your meals. Finally, you will have to make better choices about between meal snacks and the beverages that you drink.

These are just a few examples of the supporting choices that come into play when you decide to achieve a big goal. As you learn more about the power of choice, you will increase your ability to make them work using your primary and supporting choices.

The Choice Test—As Easy as 1-2-3!

One of the most important aspects of choice making is determining the quality of the decisions that we make. I developed a "Choice Test" that I use to maximize the quality of my choices and minimize the number of bad choices that I make. No, I do not use this test for every single choice that I make. However, I make certain that I use it often.

The test is simple. I just ask myself three questions about a choice I am considering. If the answer is "Yes" to any of the three questions, I make a different choice! Here are the three questions that can help you pass the "Choice Test" every time:

1. Does this choice violate any laws—natural or civil?
2. Will this choice harm me or endanger my life or the life of another person?
3. Will this choice prevent me from reaching or getting closer to the achievement of an important personal or professional goal?

That is it! It really is that simple. I have these questions written out on a small card that I keep in my wallet. These questions can help you quickly think through any important choice or decision that you need to make. However, do not allow the simplicity of this system fool you. It works and it has saved me a lot of pain and frustration that could have resulted in my life if I had not used this technique to make better choices.

The Secrets of Choice Power

I have been thinking and writing about the power of choice for many years. Now, I would like to shift the focus of this chapter to some of the most important lessons that I have discovered about the power of choice. I call them the Secrets of Choice Power because I did not learn about ideas like this during my school years. You did not either! The only place to learn them is the school of "hard knocks" or, in a book like this. Some of these ideas have had a dramatic impact on my life and my family members. I know they will benefit you and your life.

Secret #1

**The power of choice is like gravity. It always works.
The only question is "Will you be happy with the result?"**

The law of gravity is a scientific fact. Sir Isaac Newton discovered this universal truth centuries ago. It always works and it cannot be disputed. Anyone who is crazy enough to stand on top of a thirty-story building and say they do not believe in the law of gravity will learn this lesson the hard way if they jump, won't they? That person can disagree with the law of gravity all the way to the ground, but the law of gravity will work—it always works!

The power of choice works the same way. You can disagree with the fact that the power of choice is your greatest power, but it will not change anything. You can disagree with the fact that your choices determine almost everything in your life. Your choices will still make you succeed or fail. They will make you happy or sad. Yes, you need to respect the power of choice. Use this great power carefully so that you will be happy with the results.

Millions of people learn about the power of choice in the same way. They make a bad choice, one that harms them, and they pay for it over and over. People like this rarely acknowledge the impact that a bad choice can have on their life. Instead, they blame their circumstances on bad luck or society—anything but themselves and their choices. Many of our choices have the potential to change our lives forever. Our choices can affect us positively or a negatively, or they can be a neutral. Do not play games with the power of choice; believe in the power of destiny and use it wisely. Your life and your future depend on it!

Secret #2
If you do not control your choices, somebody else will.

Your choices are always under control, either yours or someone else's. The best way to retain your personal freedom and independence is to retain your Choice Power. The power of choice is not written into our Constitution, but it is actually our first freedom. When you think about it, freedom is just the power of choice in action. Guard and protect your Choice Power like you would your most valuable possessions; it is far more important than anything you can ever put in a safe!

The people with the greatest personal power and the greatest personal freedom are always the ones who make their own choices. Our individual freedoms are guaranteed by the United States Constitution. Our forefathers fought and died for this inalienable right—the right to choose! However, it is up to us to use this great gift. When we fail to control our choices, we are giving up the freedom that we are so fortunate to have. Make sure that you are the person who controls your choices and you will be in control of your life. The bottom line is this: if you want to be in charge of your life, you must be in charge of your choices.

Secret #3
Too many people base their choices on limitations, not possibilities.

I recently heard Linda Ronstadt's song, *"You're No Good"* on the radio. It made me think about the millions of people who are living with thoughts like this in their minds. The idea that they were "no good" may have come from parents, siblings, teachers, coaches—who knows?

The fact that grown adults continue to hang on to such thoughts is disappointing because this kind of negative programming has a significant impact on a person's life. No wonder there are millions of people running around telling themselves things like:

- I can't
- I'm too old
- I'm too young
- I'm too skinny
- I'm too fat

Expressions like this are perfect examples of what happens when we are programmed negatively. You have the power to re-program yourself with one-hundred-percent new programs if you choose! If you want to make Choice Power work for you, you must learn to program yourself positively. Then you will learn to make choices that expand your possibilities instead of limiting them. Remember, you have the power to make your choices and your choices have the power to make you. Choose to make your choices from a foundation of strength and possibilities instead of weakness and limitations.

Secret #4
You cannot always control your circumstances, but you can always control your choices.

Circumstances should not control your choices; your choices should control your circumstances. How many times have you heard the expression "Life is not fair?" Who said that life was fair anyway?

I have encountered many people who felt that they could do better in life if they had been born under better circumstances. You know the old saying, "The grass is always greener on the other side." Too many people spend their time thinking of ways to change their circumstances instead of creating solutions to their present situation.

I have learned that the people who truly possess the power of choice do not care about the circumstances that could be or should be; they deal with life as it is! They learn to make the best out of what they have, despite their circumstances.

Does the name Shaquem Griffin sound familiar to you? If you are not a football fan, you probably do not know the story of this courageous young man. He lost his left hand at the age of four. It proved to be a challenge that limited his physical ability in many ways. However, thanks to his wonderful parents, coaches, and the support of his twin brother Shaquill, he became a college football player at the University of Central Florida. Then, he became a linebacker in the National Football League. Yes, Shaquem learned to make the best of his situation as he overcame incredible circumstances to reach his goal of becoming a professional football player.

Shaquem Griffin did not let his physical circumstances control his choice to be a professional football player. He understood that his circumstances did limit him, but he made choices that allowed him to make the best of what he had. He knew that he probably would not be able to be a quarterback or a wide receiver in football. But he was fast and strong and he could tackle. Yes, he could tackle! Shaquem is living proof that what happens to you in life is never as important as what you choose to do about it.

Secret #5

The power of choice works just as well for a bad choice as it does for a good one.

The power of choice does not censor any of our choices—that is our job. Whatever we choose to do is acted upon automatically. This means that our greatest power can be our greatest friend or our greatest enemy. As I said earlier, our choices can imprison us or empower us.

A choice to drink alcohol at a young age can develop into a powerfully negative force in a person's life. It can lead a person down the road to a miserable life. Sadly, the power of choice will never stop itself, even if it leads to self-destruction! However, a new choice can work!

The power of choice is our greatest responsibility. It will always be like this unless we give this power to someone else. Of course, I have already advised against the wisdom of giving this power to anyone else. This means that we must become skilled at assessing the consequences of our choices before we make them so that we can choose wisely. Once we make a choice, we must live with the results. When we understand the way Choice Power works, we begin to master its true power. The simple fact is this: the choices that you make today will be the realities that you live with tomorrow.

Secret #6

Good choices made yesterday do not guarantee good choices today.

Life comes at us one second and one choice at a time. Remember, you are a living, breathing, walking, talking choice making machine. You start making choices when you get out of bed and you do not stop until your head hits the pillow again. The good choices that you made yesterday do not guarantee anything for today. They only put you in position to make more good choices in the next twenty-four hours. The worst thing that we can do is take this great power for granted. We must treat each new day as an opportunity to make more good choices; the process never ends until we take our last breath.

Successful choices in the past can be wiped out by one bad choice—instantly. Yes, even a small "bad" choice can make a big difference in your life. I never met a person who said that he or she wanted to grow up to be a drug addict or an alcoholic, but I know there are lots of adults who end up in this condition.

Either these people did not know about the power of choice or they knew about it but failed to respect it. Maybe they did not know that good choices have to be made over and over again.

Alcoholics Anonymous (AA) is a perfect example of how life, and the power of choice, works. The key to the AA rehabilitation program is to live life one day at a time. This program does not teach their members to attempt to quit alcohol forever. Instead, they teach people how to do it for twenty-four hours at a time. This is why they have been so successful for so many years. Yes, this is how you can be successful with the power of choice. Keep making good choices day by day and you will position yourself to live your best life—one choice and one day at a time!

Secret #7
When you choose a road, you also choose a destination.

The reality of making choices is remarkably simple. Every choice we make has a consequence that goes along with it. I call this reality the Law of Consequences. Every choice we make, or do not make, has a consequence. The consequence can be good or it can be bad; it all depends on the type of choice we are making. Even doing nothing is a choice that has a consequence. The advice that we all heard as children, "Look before you leap," is the kind of thinking that should accompany your choice making. If you take time to think about the consequences of a choice you are contemplating, you may choose a different path if the result will not get you where or what you want.

A perfect example of the Law of Consequences came during the Christmas season in December 2006. Our second oldest granddaughter, Katie, then age eight, was in the living room with her four-year-old sister Jessica. Young Jessica was touching the Christmas stockings that were hung on the fireplace mantle. The stockings were hanging on four heavily weighted hangers that spelled the word NOEL. Mom and Dad told the children that they could look at their stockings, but that they were not to pull on them, since they might get hurt if one of the metal hangers fell.

As Katie was reminding her sister of the consequences of pulling on a stocking, Jessica pulled on her stocking and the letter "E" came crashing to the floor and bounced into Jessica's leg. Jessica immediately started to cry from the forceful blow. Katie's warning had been ignored. So, she reminded her sister that "Gravity can be cruel."

Yes, consequences can be cruel, very cruel! It's a constant challenge to make good choices and get the results that we want instead of the things we do not want. Sometimes we may not have all the information to make the perfect choice. It all depends on the amount of risk we are willing to accept on every choice.

The reality of Choice Power is that it is all up to us; it is our responsibility to make our choices and accept the consequences that result. It is an awesome power that we must use carefully. Always remember that the Law of Consequences is just like the Law of Gravity. The law works even if you don't believe it to be true.

To Choose or Not to Choose? That is the Question

I wrote a short poem many years ago that I use to keep my mind focused on Choice Power. It reminds me that every day is a new day with new choices to be made. Check it out:

> Every morning when I get out of bed,
> I can control the thoughts in my head.
> If I want to be sad and have a bad day,
> I'll soon discover that I'm on my way.
> But if happiness is the way that I want to go
> Then the power of choice will make it so!

I call this my Choice Poem. I repeat it in first person at the start of every day and it helps me to choose the best attitude and the best thoughts that I possibly can, even in the worst circumstances. This poem is a constant reminder that I have the power to choose my thoughts and everything else that I do every day! You have the same power. I hope that you will use my Choice Poem to remind you that a life of choice is the most powerful way that you can live.

How to Increase Your Choice Power

Here are twelve guidelines that I have found helpful in increasing my Choice Power. I know that they will help you improve the quality and quantity of your choices. Try the ones you think will work for you. I am confident that these ideas will help you get the maximum benefits out of your greatest power, Choice Power—the power of destiny!

1. Begin every day with a decision to be in charge of all the choices that you will make in the next twenty-four hours. Remember you are the person that ultimately must live with your choices, so you should be the person who makes them. When you control your choices, you gain more control over your life.

You can put my Choose Poem on your bathroom mirror or on your dresser so that you can say it first thing every morning. You can also repeat the following phrase throughout the day by making your own power card to carry with you.

I AM IN CHARGE OF MY CHOICES
I AM IN CHARGE OF MY LIFE
I ALWAYS HAVE THE POWER OF CHOICE

2. Strive to make as many good choices as you can possibly make during the next twenty-four hours. This does not mean that you must make perfect choices. That is impossible and unrealistic. You can, however, work to make more choices that empower you and fewer choices that imprison you or set you back in life. Most importantly, take it one day at a time. The more quality choices you make, the better your quality of life will be for you and your family.

3. Use the Choice Test often to check the quality of your choices. Remember, the quality of your choices will ultimately determine the quality of your life. Ask yourself three simple questions before you go forward with some of the big choices in your life. First, does this choice violate any laws—manmade or natural? Second, will this choice allow me to reach or get closer to a personal or professional goal? Third, will this choice harm me or endanger my life or the life of another person? That's all there is to it. The three questions can help you think through any choice you need to make. If you say "yes" to any of the questions, just say "no" to the choice. If you don't make choices that fail the choice test you will put yourself in position to live your best life—a life of choice!

4. Make your choices from a foundation of what you can do, not from what you cannot do. Remember, too many people make their choices based on their limitations instead of their strengths. Choices that are based on your possibilities and potential are the ones that will help you be and do your best. Make the choice to "go for it" whenever you can. You can do great things if you only believe that you can. Choice Power can help turn your dreams into reality, so do not stop yourself before you even start.

5. Set personal goals and review them frequently. The people who have the hardest time making choices are the ones who do not know where they are going. Choices are always easier to make when your life has focus and direction. Goals are simply choices that are made in advance. Our lives get a lot more focused when we have goals—period! Frequent review of your goals will reinforce your efforts to make good choices and decisions that will strengthen your efforts to reach your goals. More on this in Chapter Three.

6. Have confidence in your ability to make good choices. If you have not made a lot of your own choices up to this point in your life, do not worry about it. Start where you are and go from there. Experiment with routine choices and you will gain the confidence to make bigger choices. Each good choice that you make gives you the confidence to make more and more of your own choices. Eventually, you will be making all your own choices (unless you are in a relationship—some choices need to be a "team effort") and you will exert more control over your life.

7. Always respect the power of choice. We make hundreds of choices every day. It is easy for us to take this wonderful power for granted. Do not fall into this trap. Guard your Choice Power like you would guard your most important possessions. Remember, what seems like a small choice can be a life changing event. We are always one choice away from changing our life for better, or worse. Never underestimate the power of choice because it truly is the greatest power in the universe.

8. Limit your choices when you are angry! There is only one choice to make when you are angry. That choice is to cool off! This is absolutely the best choice you can make because it may keep you from doing or saying something that could have a negative impact on your life, or someone else's. After all, ANGER is only one letter short of DANGER. Choice Power gives us the opportunity to exert the maximum control over our lives. However, you cannot be in control of your choices if you are not in control of yourself. Strive to be in control of yourself and you will always put yourself in position to make the best possible choices for yourself and other people.

9. Choose to make the best out of every situation. What happens to you is never as important as what you choose to do about it. You cannot always control your circumstances, but you can always control your reaction to your circumstances. Sometimes, success disguises itself as failure. Most people let their circumstances stop them before they ever get started. Strive to be like Shaquem Griffin and make the choice to make the best out of your circumstances. You may be amazed by the results.

10. Use supporting choices to support your primary choices. Remember no choice stands alone. Choices, like people, need support. A choice to get straight A's in school during the next marking period must be supported by good choices concerning study time, time with friends, time for sports, recreation, and study habits to name a few. Work to make your choices and work harder to find the support to make your choices work.

11. Respect the Law of Consequences and use it to improve the quality of your choices. The Law of Consequences says that every choice and every decision has consequences. Sometimes those consequences are good and sometimes they are bad. The ability to recognize the results that will follow a certain decision is a gift that can help you avoid considerable pain and discomfort. Use the Law of Consequences wisely and it will keep you from going down bad roads with bad destinations. Stay on the path that will take you to your dreams and goals. You will not be sorry!

12. Choose Excellence. One choice habit that can do more to build the life of your dreams is the choice to be and do the best you can—every day! If you can frame your choices around what it will take to do your best, you will always put yourself in position to be more and achieve more. The words of Dr. Martin Luther King, Jr. always resonate when I think about a life of personal excellence:

"If a man is called to be a street sweeper, he should sweep streets even as a Michelangelo painted, or Beethoven composed music or Shakespeare wrote poetry. He should sweep streets so well that all the hosts of heaven and earth will pause to say, here lived a great street sweeper who did his job well." (https://www.goodreads.com/quotes/21045-if-a-man-is-called-to-be-a-street-sweeper)

When you make it a habit to give the world your best, life will reward you in ways that you cannot even imagine and some that you can. I honestly believe that if you live your life in this manner, you will live a rich and fulfilling life—period!

CHAPTER 2

CHOOSE TO MANAGE YOUR MIND

> *The greatest discovery of my generation is that men*
> *can change the outer aspects of their life*
> *by altering their inner attitudes of mind.*
> —Dr. William James

William James was ahead of his time in many, many ways. He certainly had a complete grasp on the important role that the human mind plays in the creation of a great life. Author Napoleon Hill had a similar take on this important topic. In fact, he once said, "If you fail to control your own mind, you may be sure you will control nothing else." (5 Essentials, Hill, Page 101) In Mr. Hill's view, no man, or woman, can even think about being rich, or successful, if they cannot control their own mind!

Dr. James and Napoleon Hill believed in something that I call "Mind Power." Mind Power is the habit of thinking and controlling mental focus. It allows individuals to consistently produce the best possible results in their daily lives It is the ability to think good thoughts when things are going well and to think even better thoughts when things are not going well.

Mind Power is the habit of "power thinking." It is the tendency to be more optimistic than pessimistic. It is the ability to think positively and powerfully. And that is just the beginning of how our amazing minds can work if we know the secrets of Mind Power. Our minds are the critical key to self-mastery because if we do not master our own thinking, we will never be able to win the greatest battle in life—the battle of self-control. Yes, our minds are a powerful force that we must learn to master if we are to become successful and live abundantly.

Lao-Tsu, an Eastern philosopher, stated our challenge perfectly when he said, "He who controls others may be powerful, but he who has mastered himself is mightier still." The battle for self-control and riches begins in the mind. I was first introduced to the concepts of Mind Power and mental control when I read Dr. Norman Vincent Peale's classic book, *The Power of Positive Thinking*. I was twenty-six years old when I read that great book and the impact that it had on me was incredible. I had completed twelve years of basic education and six years of college, but I had never read such a powerful book. A few months after reading Dr. Peale's book I wrote the following poem:

Mind Power

A person's wealth begins in his mind.
Negative thinking really drags you behind.
When you say, "I can't do it" all day and all night.
You will soon discover, you're exactly right.
The mind is a computer–it takes what you give it,
And once you decide, you must live it.
To this great mystery there is just one solution.
You must put an end to your mental pollution.
Start doing some thought and mind rearranging.
Your life can be different if your thinking is changing
If you think lots of good thoughts and very few bad,
Then each day you live will be the best you can have.
You have great powers and genius inside,
But to use them you must decide.
Your life can be rich, or it can be poor.
You will get what you think about and nothing more!

Why is Mind Power So Important?

I believe that the human mind is the perfect power source. It is the greatest resource we possess as people and as a nation. Author Darren Hardy captured one of my favorite Napoleon Hill quotes that states "More gold has been mined from the thoughts of men than has been taken from the earth." (Hardy, Page 10)

Unfortunately, the human mind does not come with an owner's manual. To make matters worse, our schools do not teach young people how to manage their minds and get the most out of their thoughts. The result is that millions of gifted people go through life using only a small percentage of their mental gifts and potential.

Mind Power is important because it is the key that can unlock the great power and genius within each of us. Dr Peale's book taught me that we can choose to exercise complete control over one thing in this life, our thoughts! Yes, the human mind is an incredibly powerful tool. However, unless it is controlled and used wisely, it will never allow us to reach our true potential. Bottom line—many things can happen to us when we lose control of our thinking and all of them are bad!

Understanding how your mind works and learning how to use it effectively are critical to being and doing your best. Mind Power will not allow you to do anything beyond your capability, but it will enable you to do more things to the best of your ability if you use it properly. Let's find out why this is true.

Positive Thinking and Mind Power

I am often asked in my lectures and seminars if Mind Power is just a new way of thinking positive. I must admit that positive thinking is an important part of the Mind Power process, but it is just the tip of the iceberg. Unfortunately, positive thinking is misunderstood by many people and is often criticized as an unrealistic way of looking at the real world. Many people do not understand positive thinking. So, they reject it by saying that it is irrelevant and impractical in today's world.

I think people reject positive thinking for two reasons. First, they accuse positive thinkers of viewing the world through rose colored glasses Detractors say that positive thinkers simply ignore all the problems they are faced with and go happily on their way. Second, positive thinkers already have great lives. So, of course they are positive and optimistic about life. Critics believe that if "positive people" had real problems, they would not be so upbeat about life! To these criticisms I simply say, "Hogwash!"

Positive thinkers are not specially gifted people who are shielded from the despairs of depression, poor health, and broken dreams. Everyone has problems. That is a fact! The difference between positive and negative thinkers is one of focus. A positive focus helps us bring out the best in ourselves and allows us to make the best out of what happens in life.

Unfortunately, positive thinking will not allow us to do anything that we do not have the physical and mental ability to achieve. Fortunately, it will allow us to do our best in everything that we can do. Remember what we learned about our greatest power—the power of choice? Positive thinking is simply a choice: a choice to focus on the positive instead of the negative. It is a habit of focusing on solutions instead of problems. It is an attitude that allows one to view life with more optimism and less pessimism.

Life is all about choices and none of our choices are as important as the thoughts that come in and out of our mind. We always have a choice about which way we view our circumstances and what we are going to do about them. Dr. Jack Addington, the author of *Psychogenisis: Everything Begins in Mind,* expressed it best when he said, "The most important thing that you can learn in this life is that you alone choose your thoughts and your thoughts shape your world." (Addington, Page 18) What a powerful concept!

Mind Power and Attitudes—The Critical Connection

Mind Power is all about controlling our attitudes, our thinking, and our mental focus. Merriam Webster's dictionary says attitude is "A mental position with regard to a fact or state; a feeling or emotion toward a fact or state." (Merriam-Webster, Page 74) Our mental positions tend to be classified as positive or negative—optimistic or pessimistic. Attitudes are developed through our unique experiences and education within the environment that we grow up in. Eventually, they become habits of thinking that control the way we choose to view the world. Attitudes are like mental filters that process every thought and event that occurs in our life. They are critical mechanisms that exert great control and power over our thoughts and our life.

As we learned in Chapter One, the power of choice is our greatest power. The true test of how we use this great power is reflected in our thinking. We process thousands of thoughts every day. Imagine how powerful this process can be for the person who consistently thinks in a positive, optimistic manner. Conversely, think about how damaging this concept is for the person who is in the habit of thinking in a negative, pessimistic manner. Even if every circumstance and event were exactly the same for both of these people, they would lead remarkably different lives, wouldn't they? Yet, the only difference would be attitude. As William Shakespeare said, "There is nothing either good or bad, but thinking makes it so."

Positive Thinking is Good, but Power Thinking is Better

I became a positive thinker at age twenty-six. I was teaching seventh grade geography and physical education at the time. One week, I was preparing my students for a test that covered one of our biggest units of the year. We reviewed the material carefully and I drilled my students thoroughly. I was confident that everyone would do very well. I ended each review lesson by encouraging my students to "Think positive and you will get positive results."

On the day of the test, I greeted my students and told them how well they were going to do. Everyone seemed to be genuinely excited. I felt that they were ready for their best effort. One boy, however, wasn't buying this positive thinking stuff. I asked him if he was thinking positive and he said, "Yes, Mr. Gallagher, I'm positive I'm going to flunk this test." I asked, "How can you be so negative about the test?" He confidently replied, "Because I didn't study!"

That's when I realized that I needed to explain a little more about the connection between thinking and action. Thinking without action leads us to false hope and frustration. This little episode led me to the discovery of a concept that I call "Power Thinking." Power Thinking is the habit of mental management that converts negative events and circumstances into positive results through enthusiastic effort. Power Thinking starts where positive thinking ends.

As I said earlier, the concepts in this chapter are some of the most powerful ideas in this book. The power of choice is still your greatest power, but mind power and power thinking are critical to your ultimate success. Remember, your mind processes thousands of thoughts per day. Make sure that these thoughts help you to bring out the best in yourself and others. The dynamic impact of power thinking can be better understood when we examine the letters behind the word **POWER.** Each of these letters represents another word, or words, that hold an important key to this exciting concept.

Possibilities

Optimism

Way Finding

Effort

Responsibility

Now, we will take a closer look at the five concepts that drive **POWER Thinking**.

Possibilities

Power thinking is a habit of thinking that puts the focus on the possibilities, not the problems. It is the ability to look for the opportunities in a situation not at the obstacles.

I first learned about this type of thinking from the great television evangelist Dr. Robert Schuller. He was a protégé of Dr. Norman Vincent Peale, the father of "positive thinking." Dr. Schuller used his own brand of "possibility thinking" to enrich the lives of millions of people during his fifty-year ministry. I first read his "Possibility Thinker's Creed" in his book titled *Tough Times Never Last, But Tough People Do*. This creed is a constant reminder to focus our thinking on the possibilities, not the problems! Here is Dr. Schuller's classic affirmation of possibility thinking:

When faced with a mountain I WILL NOT QUIT!
I will keep on striving until I climb over,
find a pass through, tunnel underneath,
or simply stay and turn the mountain into a
GOLD MINE, with GOD'S HELP! (Schuller, Page 119)

Yes, possibility thinkers look for the possibilities in every problem instead of the problems in every possibility. This is a powerful way to approach life. It is the first key to Power Thinking.

Optimism

Optimism is the second key—a vital ingredient of power thinking. If people have hope, they have a chance to change their circumstances from negative to positive. Without hope, every person on earth is doomed to a life of emptiness and frustration. Psychological therapist, Alan Loy McGinnis researched this important topic in his book *The Power of Optimism*. He felt that optimism was frequently misunderstood, but believed it helped people make the best out of their lives. McGinnis wrote that "Optimists have not only been shown to be healthier, involved in happier marriages, and more affluent, they even live longer than non-optimists." (McGuiness, Page 176)

Optimism, like positive thinking, is usually misunderstood and often criticized as unrealistic. Once again, what makes a focus on the negative side of life more realistic than a positive focus? A six-inch glass with three inches of water in it can be described as half empty or half full. It is a matter of focus and a matter of choice, isn't it?

Optimists simply choose to focus on solutions, even if they are only partial solutions, instead of being overwhelmed by problems. This approach will always allow people to get the best out of themselves and make the best out of their circumstances. Optimism gives everyone the ability to think with power and to find the best in themselves and their circumstances. It is a vital element of the power thinking process. William Arthur Ward summarized it best when he wrote that "A cloudy day is no match for a sunny disposition." Optimists know how to make their own sunshine and they make their lives much better because of this powerful method of thinking.

Way Finding

The third key to power thinking is what I call "way finding." Way finding is the ability to solve problems. Way finding is essential to success because everyone has problems. Unfortunately, many people do not learn to find ways to solve problems. Instead, they learn to find excuses for not solving them or making things worse!

When we are posed with a problem, we have two choices: We can *find a way* or we can *find an excuse*. Again, the choice is always up to us. Power thinking helps us to find a way and it can give us the creativity, the strength, and the inspiration we need to solve the toughest problems that life has to offer. Power thinking enables us to open our minds to solutions and opportunities that negative thinking and pessimism keep hidden from our view.

Harry Houdini, the famous escape artist, pointed out this fact when he said, "Most locked doors are in your mind." The process of "way finding" can keep us from locking the doorways of our mind. It's the key that helps us find ways over, under, around, or through the obstacles that we face. It is the same key that has been used by all the great inventors and business giants for centuries.

Effort

Power Thinking does not just happen. It takes mental, physical, and emotional effort to produce the powerful results that can be generated by this type of thinking. This explains why so many people denounce positive thinking. They think lots of positive thoughts, but they do not back them up with any enthusiasm or action. This is the biggest difference between Power Thinking and positive thinking.

Power Thinking is hard work because it is so easy to get caught up in all the negative things that are going on around us. I compare this effort to swimming upstream. Have you ever tried to swim against the current? It is tough, isn't it! Power Thinking takes the same kind of effort and determination. One of my most popular lectures is titled, "How to Stay Positive in a Negative World." I use this topic to point out all the negative forces that we battle every day in our media, our workplaces, our schools, and our language, to name a few.

Just like Abraham Lincoln, I believe that people can be as positive as they make up their minds to be. The only way to get good thoughts out of your mind is to put large quantities of good thoughts in. You must think positive to be positive. You must think big to be big. You must think powerfully to be powerful. Do you get the picture?

Yes, Power Thinking takes effort. It is just like growing a garden. You will not harvest anything that you don't plant. Make the effort to fill your mind with possibilities and optimism. You will become an expert at way finding and Power Thinking. As I said in my Mind Power poem, "Your life can be rich, or it can be poor. You'll get what you think about and nothing more!" Power Thinking will not work on you unless you work on it.

Responsibility

The final key to Power Thinking is responsibility. Responsibility is the habit of being accountable for our actions and our obligations. It is also the habit of being accountable for our thoughts.

As children, we usually do not have much control over our thoughts or actions. The entire process of growth and maturation is about improving in these two areas. Remember, our thoughts and our choices are the only things that we truly have control over in the game of life.

We must accept the responsibility for our thoughts and actions if we are to be free. People who understand and accept this concept gain a sense of power and personal control that is hard to describe. We can't be in charge of our lives until we learn to be responsible for every thought that enters and leaves our mind. Publius Syrus said, "A wise man will be the master of his mind, a fool will be its slave." We will never learn to master our lives until we learn to master our thinking.

Now you know the importance of possibilities, optimism, way finding, effort and responsibility in getting the most out of your thinking and your life. More POWER to you!

The Power of the Subconscious Mind

Dr. Joseph Murphy wrote a classic book entitled *The Power of Your Subconscious Mind*. This ground-breaking book explained how the mind worked. He gave specific instructions on how to make your mind work to your best advantage. It is kind of like an owner's manual for the mind. I learned a great deal from Dr. Murphy's writing.

One of his most significant teachings is that there is only one mind. He taught that the human mind has two levels and two different spheres of activity. The conscious level is the home of our thinking and decision making. The subconscious level is the home of our emotions and our creativity (Murphy, Pages 6-8). Dr. Murphy stressed that the most important thing to remember about the human mind is that "Whatever your conscious mind assumes and believes to be true, your subconscious mind will accept and bring to pass." (Murphy, Page 33)

Now, I will expand on that concept in more detail. The conscious mind is like the monitor we use to view the programs that are running on our computer. It allows us to think and make decisions in our physical world. However, the monitor only shows a small fraction of what goes on during any computing process.

The central processing unit (CPU) is really the brain of any computer. Most of the operations of the CPU are automatic and invisible to the user. The subconscious mind works in the same way. The real power of the human mind lies within the subconscious mind. Our conscious mind represents a small fraction of what goes on in our "perfect power source."

Have you ever heard the statement that "Most human beings use less than ten percent of their mental capabilities?" Wow! That is incredible. How is this possible? I think it is possible because so few people understand how the mind actually works. People with Mind Power learn to use the limited power of the conscious mind as well as the unlimited power of the subconscious mind.

Our subconscious mind is a perfect power source that is preprogrammed to make our body function automatically. We do not have to tell our heart to beat, or our blood to circulate. In fact, in crisis situations, people have accomplished incredible feats of strength because they acted first, instead of taking time to think the situation over. In an interview that I saw many years ago, Charles Garfield, author of *Peak Performance*, told a story about a grandmother in Florida who lifted a car off the ground so that her grandson could be rescued from a near-fatal accident.

A similar situation was reported by soldiers in Vietnam who were ambushed in their jeep. These desperate men jumped out of the jeep, picked it up, and turned it around so that they could escape the ambush. And yet, they could not repeat the effort when they were challenged to prove their story to their fellow soldiers back at their base camp.

Impossible you say? Not with the subconscious mind! The previous examples prove that the mind is capable of super-human feats especially when it runs on automatic. Dr. Murphy believed that the ability to control our thinking was essential to harnessing the incredible power of the subconscious mind. He emphasized that most of the great people of any generation, especially the creative geniuses, had a deep understanding of the workings of the human mind.

We have the power to direct the subconscious mind with our thoughts and our words. The conscious mind is the master and the subconscious mind is the servant. We are in charge of this powerful machine—the machine is not in charge of us! However, we must be careful with this process because the subconscious will create anything that we order it to do. Personally, I think that everyone should have a small sticker on their forehead that reads "User Beware!" Okay, that is extreme! However, the subconscious mind is absolutely nothing to fool around with!

The Secrets of Mind Power and Power Thinking

Here are eight more important concepts that need to be developed in this chapter. The following secrets will give you more insight into the importance of Mind Power. They will help you understand the critical role that Mind Power plays in your life. They will also give you more valuable ideas that will help you get the best out of your thoughts and yourself!

Secret #1
Your mind is always under control, either yours or someone else's.

If you do not control your thinking somebody else will! This is one of the most important secrets in this book. As I mentioned earlier, it takes tremendous effort to control your thinking and to keep it focused on the things that will help you be and do your best. Have you ever had a great idea and shared it with someone who laughed at it and told you that you couldn't possibly do it? You do not need this kind of advice! It is important to know what to do when you are exposed to this kind of "Stinkin Thinkin."

If you study the life of any great person, you will discover that he or she learned this secret before they attained their success. Conversely, there are millions of talented people who settled for less in life because they let other people do their thinking for them. I know that you would not allow anyone to walk into your home and dump a big bag of garbage on your living room carpet. Yet, we let other people dump mental garbage on us every day without a second thought.

When someone tells you that you cannot do something, you have two choices. You can agree with them and stay where you are, or you can disagree with them and move forward. When you listen to the limitations and negative input of other people, you are, in fact, giving them control over your thoughts—do not do it!

If your ideas are sound, and honor the rights of others, you should stand by them and give them your best effort. This is how you control your thoughts and how you, ultimately, control your life. In my Mind Power poem, I said that we "Must put an end to our mental pollution." I believe that we should guard our thoughts like our most-valued possessions. Nobody can make us feel negative without our consent. We must always guard against the negative influences of other people on our thinking and our life. Make sure that you are the one in charge of your thoughts and you will be in charge of your life!

Secret #2

**The subconscious mind does not censor.
It works the same for good ideas as it does for bad ones.**

Censorship is a topic that gets a lot of visibility these days. Our movies, our music, our books, and our television programming are subject to the influence of censoring agencies.

Censoring devices are now available for our televisions that help parents lock out any adult programming that contains blatant sex, violence, or vulgar language. However, despite all the great capabilities of the subconscious mind, it does not come equipped with any sort of censoring equipment beyond our conscience. That is why it is so important to understand how the mind works. Again, according to Dr. Murphy, the conscious mind is the gatekeeper for the subconscious mind.

One of the chief functions of the conscious mind is to protect the subconscious mind from false impressions. The conscious mind is responsible for filtering all the thoughts and images that the human mind processes. The power of choice plays a critical role in this process because the conscious mind must choose which thoughts to accept and forward to the subconscious mind, and which thoughts to reject.

The subconscious mind will work twenty-four hours a day on any idea that the conscious mind directs it to accomplish. There will be no debates, no questions—just unfailing execution. This great power is like a two-edged sword. You must always respect it and use it carefully.

The subconscious mind will work tirelessly on a bad idea that may eventually bring about pain and suffering, if that is what it was programmed to do. The good news is that it will do the same for a good idea. Once again, the most expensive computer is only as good as the information that is programmed into it. You may remember the computer science term GIGO (Garbage In equals Garbage Out). The same holds true for the subconscious mind. Keep the garbage out and put in as much "good stuff" as you can. This is how we become the best that we can be—one thought at a time.

Secret #3

The power of belief is the key to the subconscious mind.

So far, we have learned that the subconscious mind is the key to Mind Power. Now, we will find out why belief is the key that unlocks the power of the subconscious mind. Dr. Murphy pointed out that one of the basic laws of the mind is that the subconscious mind is subject to suggestion. Any suggestion or thought that the conscious mind accepts and sends to the subconscious mind will be created in our life.

French Writer Anatole France demonstrated a clear understanding of the power of belief when he said, "To accomplish great things we must not only act, but also dream; not only plan, but also believe." Yes, belief is the foundation of anything good that happens in our world. And, unfortunately, our beliefs can lead us to bad things too.

When someone accepts something as a truth, they establish a belief pattern in their mind. Whether the idea that they accept is true or not, is not important. What is important is that the belief is accepted. This is what is acted on, not the fact. The subconscious mind does not reason, it does not argue, or dispute, it just executes.

The power of belief is the key behind the placebo effect which has been proven time and again in medical experiments. A doctor can give a sick patient a medical prescription of sugar pills that look like medicine and the patient can be cured. How can something like this happen? It happens if, and only if, the patient believes in the doctor and trusts his or her judgment.

The key to the placebo effect and the subconscious mind is belief. W. Clement Stone, author of *Success through a Positive Mental Attitude*, demonstrated his complete understanding of this concept when he said, "Whatever the mind can conceive and believe, it can achieve." (Stone, Page 57) Belief is the critical ingredient in any type of achievement or new venture. Of course, belief must be based on some reality. For example, a crippled boy can think positive thoughts and really believe that he can become basketball's next Michael Jordan, but that is an impossible dream.

Sadly, there are some physical limitations that cannot be overcome by any amount of positive thinking and positive believing. However, this boy could become a great champion in one of the wheelchair athletic programs that are popular today. We must never underestimate the power of belief and the important role it plays in human achievement. Our beliefs can power us to great accomplishments through the proper use of the subconscious mind.

Secret #4

The conscious mind can only focus on one thought at a time.

The human mind has incredible power, but it also has some important limitations. Knowledge of these limitations allows us to always get the best out of our thinking process. We have already learned that the subconscious mind is a willing servant that does whatever we tell it to do—good or bad. This fact has advantages and disadvantages as we have already learned.

The greatest limitation of the conscious mind is that it can only focus on one thought at a time, unlike the subconscious mind which can simultaneously process numerous functions.

Once again, the power of choice plays a critical role in this situation. If the conscious mind can only focus on one thought at a time, we should ensure that it is used to think about ideas that can help us be and do our best, don't you think?

Do you remember the popular song by Bobby McFerrin, "Don't Worry, Be Happy"? This song is a classic example of how the conscious thought process works and what the mind is capable of. You can choose to worry, or you can choose to be happy, but it is impossible to do both at the same time. The key question is always, "What do you focus on the most?"

Secret #5

You cannot get anything good out of a bad attitude, but you will always get your best out of a positive attitude.

The primary focus of this book is to find ways to bring out the best in ourselves and make the best out of whatever happens in our life. A positive attitude is one of the best ways to do this consistently. Yes, a positive attitude can help us do everything that we do better.

We have already discussed the criticisms of positive thinking. There are millions of people in our country who believe that positive thinking is not a realistic way of viewing the world. They stand by their cynical beliefs as the most realistic view of life.

I will be the first person to admit that positive thinking, optimism, and power thinking have their limitations. This kind of thinking cannot change everything. It cannot change facts and many times it can't change circumstances. However, Power Thinking can help us control how we react to the situation, and that alone can make all the difference.

Canadian stress researcher Dr. Hans Selye said, "Attitude determines whether we perceive any experience as being pleasant or unpleasant, and adopting the right one can convert a negative stress into something positive."

Learning to focus on the positive side of any situation is a skill that is not easily learned. Too many times we get caught in the "life is not fair" trap. We question why bad things happen to us or why bad things must happen to anybody. This kind of thinking really does not help us deal effectively with any situation. Life is always throwing tough situations at us. What really determines our success in life is how we choose to deal with it.

Secret #6

First, we make our thoughts, then our thoughts make us.

The phrases listed below are examples of something that rarely happens in life. All the people quoted agreed on one of the greatest secrets of successful living. Isn't it amazing that these great people from different cultures, from different generations, and from different religions could come up with the same conclusions about the importance how and what we think?

All that we are is the result of what we have thought.
— Buddha

Our life is what our thoughts make it.
— Marcus Aurelius

As one's thinking is, such one becomes.
— Hindu Saying

I think, therefore, I am.
— Rene Descartes

There is nothing either good or bad but thinking makes it so.
— William Shakespeare

A man is what he thinks about all day long.
— Ralph Waldo Emerson

Sow a thought, reap an act.
— Author Unknown

A man is literally what he thinks.
— James Allen

We become what we think about.
— Earl Nightingale

Everything begins in mind.
— Dr. Jack Addington

Thoughts are energy, and you can make your world or break your world by your thinking.
— Susan L. Taylor

    How many of these quotes have your read before? I believe that every one of these people understood the connection between the conscious and the subconscious mind. They also understood the power of the mind to create our outer world from our inner thoughts. It is no coincidence that these people all came to the same conclusion about the impact of our thinking on the quality of our life. The importance of our thinking and the impact that it has on our lives cannot be overstated. Researchers are uncovering scientific evidence of this fact in laboratories around the country.

    However, as you can see, wise men and women have known this secret for many generations. Our thoughts affect our physical, mental, spiritual, and emotional well-being. They have the power to bring out our best or our worst. It is critical that we understand the importance of controlling this tremendous power and learning to let it work for us instead of against us. Remember, first we make our thoughts then our thoughts make us!

Secret #7
Repetition is the key to Mind Power.

Advertising knows this secret and now, so do you! This is why we see the same advertisements on television and hear similar messages on the radio, repeatedly. It is also why we can sing the jingles and recite the lines that make us laugh in a good commercial. I once read that "Repetition is the father of habit." There is a lot of truth in that statement. Repetition is also the foundation of any skill that we ever have developed in the past and will develop in the future.

We must learn to use the power of repetition to turn our subconscious mind into our greatest ally instead of our worst enemy. Earlier in this chapter, I stated that Power Thinking is like trying to swim upstream because we must overcome so much negativism in our world. The only solution to this problem is to overcome the negativism with a positive focus and positive programming. We are the programmers of our mind. Yes, we hold the key to our subconscious minds because we can control what goes in and what comes out.

Positive, optimistic thinking is the only proven way to consistently bring out our best. However, Power Thinking will not work on us unless we work on it! The best way for us to get positive, powerful ideas out of our conscious and subconscious mind is to put positive, powerful ideas in. This process must be repeated. Our bodies need daily nourishment and so do our minds. If you want to develop the habit of Power Thinking you must stay on a healthy mental diet of positive, uplifting, optimistic thoughts. Use the secret of repetition to feed your mind proper mental vitamins and you will be on your way to living a powerful life—one thought and one day at a time!

How to Increase Your Mind Power and Become a Power Thinker

Here are ten techniques that will help you increase your Mind Power and help you become a Power Thinker. I call them the "Ten Rs" of Mind Power. They will help you keep a positive focus and enable you to use your Mind Power more effectively.

1. Read. Read at least one positive, inspirational thought every day. Read blogs, self-help books, and magazines that will increase your ability to bring out the best in yourself and make the best of what happens in your life. If you are constantly filling your mind with good thoughts, the mental garbage and toxic thinking will eventually be replaced by positive attitudes and increased optimism.

2. Reach. Reach for your personal goals. Goals are powerful because they can help you **GO After Life**. It has been proven over and over that goals and positive attitudes go together. Goals give us purpose and direction. They cause us to stretch and expand our capabilities. Goals are a perfect way to keep your mind focused on worthwhile objectives. (More details in Chapter 3)

Power Thinking and positive, worthwhile personal goals form a powerful combination that can help you find your best self and create the life you desire. More on this in Chapter Three.

3. Reduce. Reduce the amount of control that other people have over your thoughts. Do this by guarding them like your most valued possessions—because they are! Take more control over the thousands of thoughts that enter and leave your brain every day. Take full responsibility for your thinking and your actions, and you will begin to live with greater personal power.

4. Reject. Reject the negative influences of other people on your life before they turn you into a reject! Learn to recognize negative people, negative ideas, negative attitudes, and avoid them whenever possible. No one can make you feel negative without your consent. You must make a conscious choice to buy into negative and pessimistic thinking. It does not just happen. The good news is you can also choose to buy into positive and optimistic thinking.

5. Remind. Remind yourself of your strengths and your abilities on a frequent basis. Use the perfect memory within your subconscious mind to your advantage. Remember your successes, not your setbacks. Concentrate on your strengths and the abilities you are developing. Be aware of your limitations, but do not let what you can't do keep you from doing what you can do!

6. Respect. Respect yourself and respect other people. Give respect and you will get it back. Also, one great commandment says it all so well: "Love thy neighbor as thyself." It is impossible to give what you do not have, so remember to always love yourself first. You must be your own best friend before you can be a friend to someone else.

7. Repeat. Repetition is the key to learning. It is also the key to Mind Power and Power Thinking. Renew your mind with positive, uplifting thoughts and ideas at every opportunity. Memorize some of your favorites by putting them on index cards or small signs. Put them in places where you can see them throughout the day. Surround yourself with ideas and thoughts that will help you develop the habit of thinking with power and optimism.

8. Reprogram. Reprogram your subconscious mind at least once a day. The best time to do this is first thing in the morning or just before you fall asleep each evening. You should never start or end a day with negative thoughts in your mind! If you spend a lot of time in a car, start converting drive time into programming time. You can play self-development recordings while you are commuting. At the end of the day, get in the habit of reading something positive before you go to sleep. This simple technique will ensure that your subconscious mind is programmed for success. This is a powerful way to increase your Mind Power and ensure that you will become a Power Thinker!

9. Review. Review your Mind Power skills on a frequent basis. Take time at the end of the day, or at least once a week, to take a mental inventory. Do you find yourself thinking more negatively or positively? Are you becoming more pessimistic or more optimistic? Do you find it easy to be positive when things are going great, but not when times are tough? Are you using Power Thinking techniques to bring out your best and make the best out of your circumstances? The most powerful thing that you can do to change your life is to change and improve the way you think.

10. Rid. Rid yourself of the "happy when" disease if you have it. It afflicts millions of people and most of them do not even know they have it. Look and listen for this terrible affliction in the number of times you say things like:

> I will be happy when I get my promotion.
> I will be happy when I get my new car.
> I will be happy when I get married.

Do you get the picture? Happiness that is postponed into the future does not usually come to pass. The best time to be happy is right now. The best way to be happy is to drop the happy when talk and think about things that make you happy now. Be a "happy now" person and make the best of every day that you live. Keep smiling, continue working toward your goals, and enjoy the journey!

CHAPTER 3

CHOOSE TO SET GOALS

*If you do not know where you are going,
you'll probably end up some place else.*
—**Yogi Berra**

Yes, Yogi Berra had a way with words. His simple, yet profound, thoughts on life and baseball gave us plenty to think about and smile about over the years. His quote about goals, or the lack of them, is one of my favorites. J. C. Penny, founder of the famous retail store chain that bears his name, also demonstrated a clear understanding of the power of goals. He once said, "Give me a stock clerk with a goal and I will give you a man who will make history. Give me a man without a goal and I will give you a stock clerk." Goals form the basis for our destiny. I use the term "Goal Power" to describe the ability to set and achieve worthwhile personal and professional goals. It is our responsibility to fulfill our destiny through the proper exercise of Goal Power.

Goal Power is taking aim at the targets that you want to hit and then taking the actions needed to hit those targets. It's a philosophy of living that says, "All great achievements start with a dream that becomes a goal to be accomplished." Goal Power is a habit of thinking that says, "I establish the direction in my life and I know where I am going." It is an important part of personal fulfillment because it helps establish the necessary focus that we need to succeed. Finally, Goal Power is an understanding that the success process begins with Goal Setting and ends with Goal Getting!

Why is Goal Power So Important?

Would you get on an airplane if you overheard the pilot say that she had no idea where she was flying that day? Or would you get on a ship and sail on the open seas if the captain stated that he had no idea where he was going to sail? Most people would answer "No" to both questions, wouldn't you? It would be foolish to begin a trip if you did not know where you were going right? Yet how many millions of people are traveling through their lives with no written goals or plans?

The story of "Alice in Wonderland" teaches us a critical point about the importance of goals and direction. In the story, Alice stopped at a crossroads to ask the Cheshire Cat which road she should take. The cat asked Alice where she wanted to go. Alice told the Cheshire Cat that she did not really care where she was going. So, the cat responded that it would not matter which way she went. Alice had no idea where she wanted to go. So, she continued to wander aimlessly throughout the story.

There are millions of people in the world wandering aimlessly through life. Is this the way that you are traveling through your life? If so, do not despair, help is on the way.

Why Don't People Set Goals?

In his classic book, *Psycho-Cybernetics*, Dr. Maxwell Maltz observed that man is, by nature, a goal-striving being. If this is true, then why doesn't everyone set goals? It is believed that only a small portion of our adult population has specific, written, goals that they work toward every day. When I taught my Successful Living classes, I always asked my students why they did not set goals. Here are some of the most popular reasons that they gave for not putting this powerful force to work in their lives:

- Nobody ever taught me
- Don't think it's that important
- It is too hard
- It takes too much time

- Don't know how
- I already tried it and it did not work for me
- Don't think I can do anything, so why try?
- People will laugh at me if I fail
- Afraid I won't reach goals that I set
- If I do succeed, people will expect more
- Stuff like that never works for me

There are certainly many more reasons why people do not set goals, but this is a fairly good sampling. The point is that people normally set their own limits and these limits usually are low. Henry David Thoreau stated that "In the long run, men hit only what they aim at." Yes, Goal Setting helps us to aim at what is important to us, and Goal Getting helps us hit the targets we aim at!

The World's Greatest Goal Setter

Have you ever heard of a man named John Goddard? Mr. Goddard has been called "The World's Greatest Goal Setter." Others, say he was the original "Indiana Jones." Personally, I like to refer to the legendary Goddard as the "World's Greatest Goal Getter."

John Goddard became famous because at the age of fifteen he sat down at the kitchen table and started writing what he called, "My Life List." He proceeded to write down a list of 127 goals that he wanted to pursue in his life. Considering his youth, Goddard's list was beyond impressive. Here is a sampling of some of his goals:

- Explore the Amazon River
- Study Primitive Tribes in the Congo
- Climb Mt. Kilmanjaro
- Photograph Sutherland Falls in New Zealand
- Explore the Great Barrier Reef in Australia
- Visit the Great Wall of China
- Swim in Lake Tanganyika
- Become an Eagle Scout

- Appear in a Tarzan movie
- Run a mile in five minutes
- Learn to play polo
- Climb Mount Everest
- Visit the Great Wall of China
- Dive in a submarine
- Read the Bible from Cover to Cover

John began working on his list in 1939 and continued until his death in 2013. According to my count, Mr. Goddard achieved 110 of his 127 goals. He also achieved 400 more goals in his lifetime. "Wow, what a life" is what I think of when I hear Goddard's name. John Goddard did not appear to have a complex system in place for his goal achievement program. He simply put the goals on his list and then did what he had to do to achieve them.

Thanks to his "Life List," Mr. Goddard lived an amazing life that took him around the world and to places that most people never dream of. His life is a testament to the power of Goal Setting. Yes, there is something magical about putting something in your head, or heart, on a piece of paper. Learn more at: https://www.johngoddard.info/

The Science of Goal Setting

Although he may not have studied the life of John Goddard, Dr. Maxwell Maltz did research in the field of cybernetics and psychology. Cybernetics is the science of communication and control theory. The name of this unique area of study comes from the Greek word meaning "steersman." Cybernetic systems function like a servomechanism that automatically processes all feedback relating to the goal or task at hand. The servomechanism processes all information that it receives and adjusts keep the system on track and on target. (Maltz, Page 18)

In 1960, Dr. Maltz created the concept of *Psycho-Cybernetics*, which he explained in his book of the same title. Dr. Maltz concluded that the human brain and nervous system function like the servomechanisms that he read about in his study of cybernetics. Maltz compared the human brain to the servomechanism. He said that the human brain functioned like a "goal-striving mechanism" that automatically works for or against us depending on the types of goals that we set. (Maltz, Page 18)

Cybernetic systems function like a servant, not a censor. They do not signal us that our goals are good or bad; they simply act to attract the positive, or negative, forces that we create in our imagination.

Our internal goal-striving mechanism works the same for the college student who is working toward a degree and the drug addict who his trying to get his next fix. This system is closely tied to the subconscious mind, which we discussed earlier in Chapter 2. Dr. Maltz taught that our goal-striving mechanism "must have a clear-cut goal, objective, or 'problem' to work upon." Once our servomechanism has a focus, it really goes to work. The mechanism starts immediately to work on a particular goal. It will automatically pursue the target until it is achieved.

The goal-striving mechanism processes all feedback that it receives along the way. If the feedback is positive, it will continue to do what it is doing. However, if the feedback is negative, it will automatically adjust and readjust until it is back on track. Dr. Maltz pointed out that this mechanism is always working in our life whether we know how to use it properly or not. (Maltz, Page 20)

The most exciting thing about the fields of cybernetics and psycho-cybernetics is that you do not have to be an expert in either one to benefit from this powerful information. All you need to do is set some written personal goals and then start doing something to achieve them. The subconscious mind will automatically function like a goal-seeking device that will take us to our goals. Yes, it is just like electricity. All you must do is flip the switch and let it work!

The Basics of Goal Setting

Now, it is time to take a closer look at the Goal Setting process. In this section, I will describe the two types of goals that we can set, the two ways to set them, and the different time periods involved in the goal setting process.

Goals are always focused in one of two areas. Goals are either internal or external. Internal goals focus on self-improvement and personal growth. External goals are focused on measurable performance and personal achievement.

Internal goals are extremely important because you build your best life from the inside out. Our internal goals help to bring out our best by improving our attitudes, skills, and abilities. The primary purpose of this book is to cause you to improve yourself so that you can achieve anything you set your mind and heart on. Internal goals can help put us in the best position to achieve the results and outcomes that we desire. Yes, internal goals are primarily focused on self-improvement.

External goals are also especially important in the overall scheme of living your best life. Our internal skills and abilities can allow us to perform at an extremely high level in the workplace, in our relationships and in matters of health and fitness. All personal achievements can be traced back to your internal habits and skills. Everything that you hope to achieve will be measured in some external way. If you want to get the best out of yourself and your life, you will have to set some external goals that focus on personal achievement.

There are two ways to set goals. The first way is to base them on past performance. This is the most "realistic" way to set goals, and many people use this method to get good results. Most beginners start their goal setting programs this way. They look at something that they have done in the past and set a slightly higher goal. The runner wants to improve his time by ten seconds in the mile run while somebody else sets a goal to lose five pounds in two months.

Another way is to base them on the decision to achieve the goal, regardless of previous past performance. This way is often criticized as "unrealistic," but this is the method that usually leads to great achievements. In 1960, President John F. Kennedy set an "unrealistic" goal when he announced to the world that America would be the first country to put a man on the moon. This same method was used by Thomas Edison to invent the incandescent light bulb.

Both methods have advantages and disadvantages, but the important point is to understand the difference when you are setting your goals. Sometimes we know what we are capable of and sometimes we just believe we can do something. Either way, goals will give us the direction and focus we need to get where we want to go in life. There are many different goal-setting programs and many different time periods attached to the goal-setting process. Here is the system that I use:

1. Lifetime Goals. Lifetime goals are the ultimate focus of our existence! They provide the direction for living, for working, and for life. It is especially important to start from where you want to end up which is why these types of goals are listed first. Author Stephen Covey called this, "Beginning with the end in mind." These goals are driven by your dreams and the ultimate vision that you want for your life. This is where John Goddard's "Life List" came from and where "Bucket Lists" originate. "What do you want to do with your life?" is the question that will help you set your own lifetime goals.

2. Long-Range Goals. Long-range goals are goals that are focused five to ten years in the future. Once again, these objectives may be stand-alone goals or they may be smaller parts of a much bigger goal. Goals like this connect our yearly goals and our lifetime goals in decade-size chunks. They keep us on course and keep us positioned to arrive at our desired future as planned.

3. Short-Range Goals. Short-range goals are goals that you are focusing on two to four years away. They may be goals entirely unto themselves or they may be smaller elements of a more long-term objective. The focus here is sharper than it is for lifetime and long-range goals. However, it is still more general than specific.

4. Yearly Goals. Yearly goals are commitments that we make to our self to achieve within a twelve-month period. Many people call yearly goals their New Year's Resolutions. However, many people fail to understand, or appreciate, the process of Goal Setting which is why they normally do not achieve their resolutions. The difference between a resolution and a goal is the level of planning, commitment, and action. Yearly goals, that are written and backed by sound plans and action, can be powerful magnets that will attract you to one achievement after another!

5. Quarterly Goals. Quarterly goals are the goals that we plan to accomplish in a three-month period. Most corporations break their yearly objectives into quarterly segments and successful people do the same. Successful people know the value of focusing their efforts on a quarterly schedule. A three-month focus gives us specific targets, but also allows for some flexibility in adjusting our objectives based on each month's progress, or lack of progress, toward the quarterly target.

6. Monthly Goals. Monthly goals are the specific goals that we plan to achieve within a period of twenty-eight to thirty-one days. The focus and direction of monthly goals is much more specific than any of the other time frames mentioned so far. Monthly goals have less to do with planning and more to do with scheduling, acting, and getting results.

7. Weekly Goals. Weekly goals are the specific activities, actions, and results that you want to achieve in a seven-day period. Weekly goals have clear direction and sharp focus. The actions can be scheduled in daily and hourly time frames. This is where plans start to get real and where the power of Goal Setting gets us focused on what is important.

8. Daily Objectives and Results. All goals eventually need to be broken down to specific tasks and actions that need be accomplished "today." Daily objectives and results are the steps and actions that must be taken to accomplish a goal or goals. To determine what your daily goals should be, ask yourself: "What do I need to do today to reach Goal X?" and "What will it take to progress toward Goal Y?"

Daily actions give us the sharp focus that is required to control our thoughts, actions, and schedules. This ensures that the maximum amount of our time is invested in the activities that we most want to achieve. Very few goals are achieved in one giant step. There is an adage that says, "The journey of one thousand miles begins with a single step." Daily actions are the small steps that we must take to progress from being Goal Setters to Goal Getters!

Goal Setting Guidelines

Now, let us examine some important concepts involved in the goal-setting process. These guidelines will help you learn how to set personal goals that will allow you be and do your best. Use these twelve guidelines to become more successful at goal setting and goal getting:

1. Goals must be personal.
2. Goals must be congruent with our values.
3. Goals should be written, specific and measurable.
4. Goals should be action-based and results oriented.
5. Goals should have a time dimension attached.
6. Goals should be stated in present tense and in positive terms.
7. Goals should cause you to stretch, but not break your spirit.

8. Goals should have long-term focus and short-term results.
9. Goals should be guarded carefully.
10. Goals should be reviewed frequently.

1. Goals must be personal. The most difficult goal to achieve is the one that someone else sets for you or one that you set for someone else. Parents do not have the right to tell a child what to do with his or her life. However, they do have a responsibility to help their offspring find direction in their lives. The best thing that we can do for ourselves and our future is to set some challenging personal goals that capture our hearts and our heads. The next best thing is to teach our children to do the same!

2. Goals must be congruent with our values. We are influenced by many forces in life, but the greatest influence is always our basic values. When we live according to our values, we eliminate personal conflict that can limit our performance and reduce our daily effectiveness. Roy Disney expressed it best when he said, "It's not hard to make decisions when you know what your values are." When we try to achieve goals that do not match our value system, we are affected negatively by the conflict. Remember, goals are just decisions, or choices, made in advance. When our decisions and choices are in synch with our values, magical things can happen!

3. Goals should be written, specific, and measurable. All written goals will answer five immensely powerful questions: Who, What, When, Where, and Why?

My research and personal experience with goal setting has taught me that there is something immensely powerful about putting a goal in writing. It goes back to what we learned earlier about the subconscious mind. The simple act of writing a goal makes it a concrete entity.

A written goal statement is the first step on the journey from dreams to reality. Goals also need to be specific and measurable so that we can focus on the results that we want to achieve.

If you say that your goal is to be a famous football player, you do not have a goal that is specific or measurable. However, if you say, "I am a twenty-three-year-old football player in the National Football League on August 31, 2023," you have a specific goal that is measurable. This sort of specificity adds clarity, focus and direction to your life.

4. Goals should be action-based and results-oriented. Goals should be written so that the desired action, behavior, or result can be measured. Instead of saying, "I will spend more time with my children," write, "I attend all my son's baseball games." or "I listen to Joey read for 20 minutes five days a week." These are actions that you can evaluate and measure because they will require specific actions to achieve the desired result. Written goals that are action-oriented and results-based give you the best chance of achieving the outcomes you desire.

5. Goals should have a time dimension. Goals need schedules if they are going to be different than wishes and dreams. No, "someday" does not cut it when you are talking about setting goals. The most successful goal setters establish realistic time frames for their goals.

This is important because if we do not establish a target date, we may lose interest or fail to develop the proper sense of urgency required to achieve our goals. A target date adds a powerful dimension to the goalsetting process and gives us another tool to focus our efforts.

6. Goals should be stated in the present tense and in positive terms. Once again, the power of a written goal statement is almost magical. Goals should be written in the present tense so that the subconscious mind starts to believe it is already being achieved. Instead of saying, "I'll lose ten pounds by June 15, 2022," say, "I weigh 146 pounds on June 15, 2022." Remember, the subconscious mind cannot tell the difference between vivid imagination and fact. Also, goals need to be written in positive terms instead of negative terms. Notice the difference in focus between these two phrases:

"I won't smoke anymore after September 15, 2023" or "I live a smoke free life as of September 15, 2023."

The big difference between these two goals is the focus, right? It is always better to think about what you want to do instead of locking in on what you don't want to do. This does not seem like a big deal, but positive words are the best way to state your goals.

7. Goals should cause you to stretch yourself without breaking your spirit. The best goals are always the ones that bring out your best. Your goals must challenge your abilities and cause you to stretch yourself to new levels. However, we must also ensure that our goals are realistic. It is important to remember that there are some things that are impossible.

The young man who will spend his entire life in a wheelchair is setting himself up for failure if he sets a goal to become a professional athlete in the National Football League. On the other hand, this person could become a radio announcer, a staff member in a professional football organization, or a sportswriter who covers college or professional football. These goals are certainly possible and would bring out the best in this young man without breaking his spirit.

8. Goals should have long-term and short-term focus. We need long-term goals in our life to get us excited and help us overcome the short-term obstacles and disappointments that we may face in our Goal Setting efforts. We also need to develop the proper short-term focus so that we can take the little actions required to achieve our goals.

Our short-term focus should be on the path that will take us to our goals. This path must be traveled one step at a time, one day at a time, and one week at a time. Long-term goals provide the vision that we need in our life and short-term actions ensure that we get there. Both are required if we are to become successful at setting and reaching our goals. My advice is simple in this area: Think big and do the little things it takes to get there!

9. Goals should be guarded carefully. Always guard your goals as carefully as you guard your most valuable possessions. It is better to keep them protected and hidden from public view than it is to risk public criticism of your dreams and plans. People do not always respond positively and supportively when we share a goal. Some people may be jealous and criticize your efforts. Others may not believe you can achieve it and do not want to see you get hurt after failing.

My advice is to carefully nurture your goals with a steady diet of positive affirmations and Power Thinking. Be cautious and only share your goals with people who will support you and encourage your efforts. The bottom line is this: Do not let anyone steal your dreams or your goals!

10. Goals should be reviewed frequently. Periodic review of your goals is essential in any goal-setting program. This effort allows you to maintain your focus and direction. Sometimes you may discover that a goal that seemed powerful and exciting a year ago has now been replaced by something more important and that's okay. Regular review of your goals will keep you on target. It also ensures that your goals still match your values, your lifetime objectives and your "bucket list" priorities.

The Dynamics of Goal Getting

Most people think they know how to write goals, but that is only part of the process. The second part of the goal-achievement process is a dynamic combination of mental and physical actions, fueled by intense desire. I believe the reason that most people fail to achieve their goals is their lack of understanding of how Goal Getting really works. The next page contains an illustration I created to portray how this dynamic process works.

There are three things that must happen in the Goal Getting process:

- First there is mental action.
- Second there is physical action.
- Third, all actions must be fueled by intense desire.

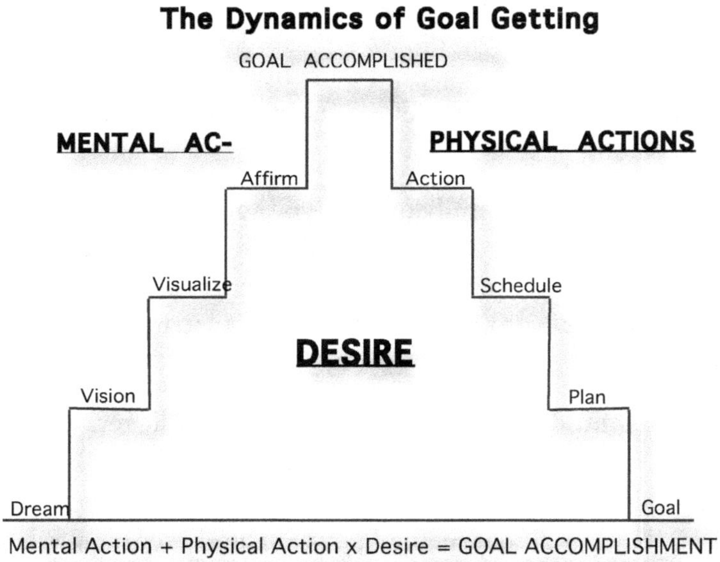

The Dynamics of Goal Getting

GOAL ACCOMPLISHED

MENTAL AC-   **PHYSICAL ACTIONS**

Affirm   Action

Visualize   Schedule

DESIRE

Vision   Plan

Dream   Goal

Mental Action + Physical Action x Desire = GOAL ACCOMPLISHMENT

Figure 3-1

This graphic illustrates the importance of everything that must occur if we are to achieve our goals. The stairway metaphor captures the challenge everyone faces as they try to get from Goal Setting to Goal Getting. As you can see, there are certain steps that must be taken in support of each other if we are to maximize our Goal Getting capabilities. I believe we must walk up both sides of the stairway, often at the same time, if we are to maximize our goal-setting efforts and successfully achieve our objectives.

This is how we develop the ability to not only set goals, but to get those goals. If you are missing any one of the three aspects of Goal Getting, you will probably fail in your efforts to achieve even the smallest goal.

The Dynamics of Goal Getting is an important concept that holds the key to a thorough understanding of the process of goal accomplishment. The model on the previous page illustrates the powerful relationship between the mental side and the physical side of the Goal Getting process.

Mental Actions are the internal activities that must occur to create our goals, internalize them, and maintain proper focus. The process starts with a dream that begins to come alive when it becomes a clear vision to be achieved. This vision is crystallized in the subconscious mind through the power of visualization. Visualization is the key to enlisting the tremendous power of the subconscious mind in the Goal Setting process. The final part of this process is to affirm your success—before you achieve it! Yes, affirmations are critical tools that can help us focus on our goals, strengthen our resolve, and program ourselves for successful goal accomplishment.

Physical Actions are the external steps that we must perform if we are to achieve our goals. First, we must bring our vision to life by expressing it as a written goal. Next, we must invest some time to develop a plan that will lead to the successful accomplishment of our goals. Then, we schedule the actions that will put us in position to achieve our goals. Finally, action, focused action, will enable us to achieve our objectives and get our goals!

Desire is the passionate "want to" that allows us to persist in our efforts and maintain our concentration and focus. We get into action by acting and doing what needs to be done. However, failure and unforeseen obstacles can distract us and defeat us if we lack the resolve to fight through the tough times. Desire adds power to our efforts and provides mental and physical persistence that is critical to our ultimate success.

Goal Getting is a dynamic process that integrates our internal and external resources and maximizes our performance abilities to achieve success. When you fuel your mental and physical abilities with the power of desire, you are in the best position to get the best out of yourself. This high level of performance will put you in the best possible position to achieve the results and outcomes that you seek in your personal and professional life.

The Secrets of Goal Power

Let us continue to explore the fascinating topic of Goal Power. The ideas revealed below provide some additional insights about the power of setting and getting goals. I call them the Secrets of Goal Power. I will bet you that you did not learn about these secrets in high school or even college. These concepts are critical to your overall understanding of the magical power of goals.

Secret #1
The only impossible goal is the one you do not have.

Mr. Jeffrey Albert made a powerful statement about goals when he said, "The first and most important thing about goals is having one." This may sound obvious to you, but there are millions of people in the world who have no idea how powerful goals really can be. Developing the Goal Setting habit is one of the best things that you can do to increase your personal and professional success.

I really believe in the power of goals, but this great power only works on us when we work on it! People who do not set goals normally fail to live up to their full potential and win big in the game of life. I do not consider myself a gambling man, but I would make this bet with anyone: You will always fail to achieve one hundred percent of the goals that you don't set. Bottom Line: You gotta have goals!

Secret #2
What counts most in life is not where you have been, but in what direction you are growing.

In 1976 I heard superstar life insurance salesman Joe Gandolfo make a startling statement about goals. He told a crowd of over ten-thousand people that "If you don't have any goals in life it doesn't really matter how long you live." Wow, I still remember his exact words after all this time! Although this statement sounds harsh, it points out the futility of living without dreams, goals, and purpose.

Age really has little to do with the goal-setting process. Tragically, young people who lack purpose often end up as suicide victims, while many elderly people die less dramatically from old age and/or a lack of purpose. I believe that a big part of old age is mental, which is why I think that people of any age can retain their vitality and motivation through the power of personal goals.

Secret #3
**A goal that you are interested in is a good goal.
A goal that you are passionate about is a great goal.**

Goals are powerful motivational forces that can cause us to be and do our best. Merely being interested in something can generate enough energy and enthusiasm to accomplish a challenging task. However, the true power of goal setting comes from what I call "Why Power." Yes, Why Power is the power of motivation.

The stronger your purpose, the stronger your motivation will be. The more "whys" and reasons you have supporting your goals, the more powerful will be your desire to achieve them. Passion, when properly directed, can power up your living and your life.

The more you care about what you are doing, the more effort you will expend to accomplish it. This helps to create the focus and desire that improves effort and practically guarantees great results. A good goal will capture our interest, but a great goal will capture our heart. The bottom line is that passion can add tremendous power to your Goal Getting efforts. It can help you turn good goals into great goals. Yes, goals are a powerful force in the world.

Secret #4
First you make your goals; then your goals make you.

This is one of the most powerful concepts in this chapter. The surest way to bring out the best in yourself and others is to set goals in a variety of areas in your life. The bigger the goals we set, the bigger and better we can become in the process. Once again, the magical part of the goal-setting process is hard to explain, but it works. Again, when I look at the word *GOAL* I see an acrostic that stands for the phrase *GO After Life*! Goals give us the power to go after life instead of waiting for life to happen to us. A balanced goals program is critical if we are to be the best person we can become. Goals have the power to stretch us and cause us to be and do our best. When we set goals, we start the dual process of using more of our physical and mental talents to achieve our objectives. Start going after your life by going after your goals. Your life will never be the same!

Secret #5
If your goal is to hunt deer, do not waste time chasing squirrels.

Goal Power is really the power of focus. This power comes from the direction and energy that goals add to our life. However, this power can be wasted if we do not remain focused on our goals.

The Goal Setting process eventually comes down to a confrontation between direction and distraction. Goals can help us overcome distractions by focusing our energy and actions on the tasks that will help us be and do our best. They can take us where we want to go, but we must be alert for the daily temptations that can take us down easier, but less fulfilling paths. Racehorses wear blinders to keep their focus on what is in front of them—the path to the finish line. You need to find ways to maintain your discipline and focus your attention on where you want to go.

One of my expressions for Goal Setting is "decision making in advance." There is magic in the physical act of writing down a clear, concise, specific goal statement. Goal statements have the power to activate the subconscious mind and energize our actions like nothing else. The key to this dynamic process is the power of focus. The important thing to remember is that distractions will always be present. However, if we are focused on our goals, we can ignore the smaller distractions and keep pursuing our bigger goals. The bottom line is this: more focus equals more goals achieved.

Secret #6
The ultimate test of any goal is one simple question: "Will this goal help me bring out my best?"

Yes, you need to ask yourself "Will this goal help me to bring out my best?" This powerful question should be asked about every goal you set. These words provide a simple tool that helps us determine if a potential goal meets the of living your best life. Goal Power is a dynamic process that requires us to think and act with purpose, direction, and focus. Any goal that passes the Goal Test" will be a good goal because it will benefit you and maybe others as well.

Conversely, any goal that fails this test is something that must be discarded immediately. I once heard motivational speaker Zig Ziglar express this concept perfectly when he said, "You can get anything in life if you just help enough other people get what they want." (Ziglar, Page 382) This approach to Goal Setting is what constitutes the ultimate approach to living. If your goals rest on this sort of a foundation, they will always pass the test and set you up to be and do the absolute best you can. You will always put yourself in position for success when your goals seek to bring out the best in yourself and other people.

Secret #7
Winners practice the habit of finding goals: Losers practice the habit of finding excuses.

Winners are always looking for new goals while losers are always looking for excuses. John Dewey pointed out that "Arriving at one goal is the starting point to another." I have observed that people who understand Goal Power also understand the value of always having a goal, regardless of age, sex, or station in life. Everyone needs goals and they need to be doing something every day to achieve them. Learn to focus more of your time on finding ways to achieve your goals and less time finding excuses for not achieving them. Remember life is a journey, not a destination.

The Goal Setting/Goal Getting process is a continuous part of a successful person's life. The achievement of one goal provides a stepping-stone to the next. This cycle can, and should, continue for a lifetime if we are to consistently bring out the best in ourselves and live our best life. Unfortunately, losers are usually far too skilled at finding excuses for not achieving their goals.

There is always a reason and it is never the loser's fault. Do not fall into this trap. Think like a winner and keep looking for new goals and new ways to achieve them. Practice this philosophy and you will be too busy, too successful and too happy to let excuses limit your thinking or your life!

How to Put Goal Power to Work in Your Life

Goal Power is one of the critical elements of the Choose and Grow Rich program. It is the primary tool we can use to stay focused and headed in the right direction. Here twelve steps that will get you started on a lifetime of achievement. These actions and procedures will help you write specific, measurable, action-based, goals that will help you be and do your best. Here is a Goal Setting/Goal Getting process that I created many years ago. Follow these steps and you will add a powerful force to your life—Goal Power!

1. Fantasize
2. Categorize
3. Itemize
4. Prioritize
5. Crystallize
6. Energize
7. Strategize
8. Visualize
9. Verbalize
10. Vitalize
11. Analyze
12. Realize

Now, we will examine each step in greater detail to help you develop a sound understanding of the entire process. You will notice how each step builds on the other and how they all work together synergistically.

1. Fantasize. The best way to begin your formal goal-setting program is to go on a dream spree. No, I am not going to give you ten-thousand dollars and instruct you to go shopping at your favorite mall. Instead, I want you to do something a thousand times more fun! Schedule thirty minutes of uninterrupted time and commit to doing one of the most exciting things you will ever do in your life Find a quiet place in your house or apartment and get five or six freshly sharpened pencils and plenty of lined paper. Now, do what John Goddard did. Write your name and "My Life List" at the top of a sheet of paper and date it. Do the same for three or four more sheets. If you need more, you can repeat, as necessary.

Think about anything and everything that you want to become, learn, do, own, visit, or experience, and start writing them down on the paper. Do not worry about spelling, punctuation, or grammar. Just write as much and as fast as you can. Do this for at least five minutes and longer if possible. Do not worry about being logical during this exercise. Let your imagination run wild! If an idea pops into your mind, write it down; you can make sense of it later. Do not think about how you're going to do anything—just write, a lot!

When you get to a point where you run out of ideas, take a short break, and start writing again. Do this until you get to the end of your thirty-minute session. I was able to write down ninety-one goals the first time I did this life-changing exercise. This project was one of the most exciting things I have ever done. You will find yourself updating and adding to your original list frequently.

Just make sure that you date each item when you add it to your list. Your "Life List" will keep you focused for many years—I promise!

2. Categorize. Now it is time to separate your "Life List" into different goal categories. Here are seven areas that are commonly used for classifying personal goals.

- Career/Professional
- Educational/Mental
- Family
- Financial
- Health/Physical
- Leisure/Recreational
- Personal Development

The purpose of this step is to organize your Goal Setting program and focus your time and energy. I am confident that everything that you wrote on your master "Life List" will fit into one of these categories. Take time to write one goal category at the top of eight sheets of paper. If you want to speed up the process go back and number every dream/goal on your list. Then, write the number of each one on a list that best describes the goal category. This keeps things moving and allows you start fast!

3. Itemize. Now, take some time to review your "Life List" and list each dream on one of the category sheets that you have prepared. Some of your dreams will overlap. They could be added to more than one list. So, do not worry too much about this. Put your dreams in the category that you want and move on. You make the call where it belongs because this is your list. Take time to list every goal on your "Life List" on an appropriate category sheet. Yes, this is tedious, but it is an important step in the process.

4. Prioritize. Once your dreams are listed on the appropriate category sheets you can start to prioritize them. Review each category list and select the top two to three dreams that you want to achieve within the next year.

Use a highlighter to capture the dreams that you will focus on initially. It is a good idea to select some of your smaller, or easier dreams, first because success is critical to building skill and developing your Goal Setting confidence. Then, look at the numbers that you wrote on the category sheets and write out the top three dreams on your list in order—1, 2 and 3! Putting priorities on your goals helps you begin the process of thinking and planning, which is critical to a successful Goal Power program.

5. Crystallize. Putting your goals in writing is the first step to making your dreams become reality. Goal statements crystallize your dreams and start to give them a life of their own. Goal statements are powerful because they answer four of the six important questions that we need to ask ourselves about our goals.

A written goal statement answers "Who," "What," "Where," and "When," about every goal that you want set. Yes, it does take some time, but it is worth it. This process will help you focus and identify the measurable outputs that you expect to achieve. Goals that are written according to this method will look like this when they are completed:

> Barry Gallagher publishes his best-selling book, *The Greatest Football Story Ever Told: Michigan vs. Ohio State 1897 to 2022* in Aurora, Illinois not later than November 30, 2022.

6. Energize. This is the next important step in the Goal Setting/Goal Getting process. It is a key part of the program because this is where you ask yourself the big "Why" question. "Why" is the fifth of the six power questions that we must ask ourselves about each goal we set. It will help you search your inner-self and discover the depth of your commitment to each goal. This is the time where you will find out if a proposed goal really fits with your values and beliefs. It will also help you discover if a potential goal is something you are merely interested in or passionate about. Now the goal on page 77 looks like this when you add the "Why:"

> Barry Gallagher publishes his next best-selling book, *The Greatest Football Story Ever Told: Michigan vs. Ohio State* in Aurora, Illinois not later than November 30, 2022 to tell the amazing story of the greatest rivalry in college sports.

7. Strategize. The seventh step in the Goal Power process answers the last of the six power questions. The final question is the "How" question. "How" helps you develop a strategy that will lead you to the achievement your goals. Remember, goals provide us with direction in life, but plans provide the path. A plan is a strategy that is put into writing. When you develop a plan for each goal that you want to achieve, you are laying the foundation for a road that will eventually take you to your goals. A well-conceived plan provides a bridge to the future by anticipating obstacles that must be overcome and forecasting actions that are required to get you to your objective. Bottom line—plans are a small investment that pays big dividends in the future. Invest the time it takes to develop a strategy and put it in writing. This is a critical key to your personal and professional success!

8. Visualize. History continues to teach us that everything that is created in this world is created twice: first in the mind of the inventor, or creator, and then in reality. Every idea starts in the mind, but that is as far as some of them get. All great inventions started out as a visualized image in someone's mind. Then, that image was created in a physical form over the course of many months or years. Remember, "What you see is what you get?" People who understand the power of visualization understand that they can be or do just about anything that they first see in their mind. Filmmaker George Lucas said it best when he stated that "You can't do it unless you can imagine it."

Visualization is not an ability that is only reserved for artists, athletes, and inventors. Everyone can use this powerful skill to support their Goal Setting and Goal Getting efforts. As we learned earlier, there are two sides to the Goal Power process: the mental side and the physical side. Visualization is a critical part of the mental side of the Goal Power process. Your Goal Setting and Goal Getting efforts will be greatly enhanced if you add this powerful ally to your personal skill set.

9. Verbalize. The way that we talk has a tremendous impact on our ability to achieve our goals. As I mentioned earlier in this chapter, there is a lot of truth in "What you see is what you get." I also believe that there is much truth in one of my favorite expressions: "What you say is what you get." The way we talk to ourselves is critical to our attitude, our self-image, and to our ability to achieve our goals. We can talk ourselves into and out of almost anything. We do it all the time.

Our words play a powerful role in the achievement of our goals. Yes, we must learn the skill of affirmations if we are to maximize our ability to set and get our dreams and goals. Affirmations are positive statements that reflect current and future conditions or facts. Affirmations serve three important functions in the Goal Power process because they:

- Program the subconscious mind with specific thoughts that it needs to help you grow towards your goals.
- Keep your conscious mind focused on the thoughts and actions that you need to concentrate on to achieve your goals.
- Develop a positive attitude about your goals and help maintain the maximum level of optimism.

Bottom line—the way we talk to ourselves is critical to everything that we think, feel, and do. We will take a much closer look at the importance of words in Chapter 4.

10. Vitalize with Action. This step is where the Goal Power process starts to get extremely exciting! Yes, the entire process of dreaming and creating goals is a dynamic process. Action is the ultimate step that we must take to achieve our goals. The small steps that we take to achieve our goals can become powerful sources of energy and enthusiasm. These actions are daily in some cases, weekly in others, and maybe only monthly for other goals. Action is what separates the Goal Setter from the Goal Getter. Goals without action are empty promises to yourself that create frustration and disappointment. With action, every goal can become reality.

11. Analyze. Once we start taking action to achieve our stated goals, we need to make periodic assessment to determine if we are making the progress we desire. I believe that all Goal Setters should take time out of each week to assess their progress towards their written goals. This is a good investment of time because it allows us to see what actions are generating the results we want and what actions are not getting us where we want to go.

12. Realize. The successful accomplishment of a worthwhile, personal goal is one of the most exhilarating events in life. It is exciting, and also very fulfilling. Each time we achieve a goal, we come to the realization that we have been given the power to make a difference in our life, the lives of other people, and the world in which we live. This is a powerful way to live. I recommend that you update your "Life List" frequently. This document will provide you with a great source of inspiration and motivation for years to come.

Here is a SMARRRT way to set goals.

Earlier in this chapter I shared ten guidelines for setting goals. Now, here is an easy way to think about setting goals. Here are the words that are usually associated with these seven letters:

Specific – Goals need to be specific not general in nature. "I want to be a movie star is a general statement" that can't be considered a goal. Here is an example of something more specific: "I begin my acting career with a supporting role in our community players presentation of *My Fair Lady* on August 1, 2023.

Measurable – A true goal must be measurable. There must be a way to determine if you have achieved the desired objective. In the previous example, the aspiring actress will be able to measure her success by the fact that she secured a role in the play that begins on August 1, 2023. Of course, if she didn't secure the role she desired she could set a new goal or move on to another one.

Actionable – The best goal statements contain verbs that indicate what needs to be done. In the first example in this section, "I want to be a movie star" is more of a wish than a goal. "begin" my acting career is an action statement that comes alive when it is linked to a definite time and place.

Read & **R**eviewed **R**epeatedly – In my system, goals must be written and read and reviewed repeatedly. I recommend that you read and repeat your goals in the morning and again before you go to bed. Such an approach gives you the opportunity to maintain the focus that you need to actually achieve a stated goal. Yes, successful goal achievement does take some work but it is worth it!

Targeted – The best goal setting systems share one final element which is a time element. A goal that is targeted to a specific date and time is more likely to be achieved.

Here is a goal statement that demonstrate how to incorporate all the SMARRRT goal elements into a desired outcome:

Barry Gallagher publishes his next best-selling book, The Greatest Football Story Ever Told: Michigan vs. Ohio State in Aurora, Illinois not later than November 30, 2022 to tell the amazing story of one the greatest rivalry in college sports.

If you take the actions that you need to take to achieve your stated goals and read them daily, you cannot fail!

CHAPTER 4

CHOOSE YOUR WORDS—CAREFULLY

> *Words are, of course, the most*
> *powerful drugs used by mankind.*
> —**Rudyard Kipling**

Yes, we need to be incredibly careful about how we use our words. A group of letters joined together can have a huge impact on other people and our lives. Rudyard Kipling's powerful quote captures the importance of words, doesn't it? Wow, he wrote that comment over one hundred years ago and it is still true today!

Motivational expert Bob Moawad believed that "Words are tools. They predict or perpetuate performance." We are exposed to millions of words in a lifetime and these words have a powerful impact on every aspect of our life. People who understand the power of words and know how to use them are the ones who will reap the benefits of Say Power. Let's find out why words play such an important role in our life and what we can do to use them as powerful tools to help us be, know, feel, and do our best.

I use the phrase "Say Power" to describe the process of making your words matter to yourself and to others. Say Power is the habit of controlling our "self-talk" and using words to consciously program yourself in a positive manner. It is the ability to bring out the best in yourself and others through the power of the spoken word. It is a way of living that says, "I understand the powerful impact that words have on my thoughts, my actions, and my self-image." It gives you the ability to take control of the words you speak to yourself and others. Finally, it is a process of consciously programming yourself for personal fulfillment through the frequent use of affirmations and positive mental programming. Say Power is a critical skill that you can use to bring out the best in yourself and make the best out of what happens in your life.

Why Is Say Power So Important?

Did you know that words have the power to raise or lower body temperature, raise and lower pulse rate, secrete hormones, and dilate and constrict arteries? Dr. Shad Helmstetter in his popular book, *What to Say When You Talk to Yourself*, estimated that by the age of eighteen most of us have been told no or what we could not do, more than 148,000 times! (Helmstetter, Page 10) He also stated that "Leading behavioral researchers have told us that as much as seventy-seven percent of everything we think is negative, is counterproductive, and works against us." (Helmstetter, Page 11)

As a parent, and former educator, I know that parents and children are not taught about the importance of programming or the power of words. Yes, we teach our children the alphabet and how to spell.

We teach them how to read and how to speak the English language. However, we fail miserably at teaching them how to program themselves for success. Very few young people understand how important it is to control their words, their thoughts, and their attitudes. We do not teach them how to reject the negative programming they receive from hurtful friends, school peers and adults.

Yes, Say Power is important. It affects us almost every waking minute of our lives. Say Power is a powerful concept that we must understand and master if we are to become the best person that we can be. The words that we say to ourselves and the ones that we hear from others have a powerful impact on our lives. It starts with the first words we hear as infants and continues until we die. Words are powerful tools that can build people up or tear them down. We must learn to use our words carefully. It is never too early, or too late, to master this important power.

Sticks and Stones May Break My Bones, But Words....

Do you remember the little rhyme that your mother used to say to you when someone said something that upset you? "Sticks and stones may break your bones, but words will never hurt you." I repeated that phrase many times as a child when other children would say mean and hurtful things to me. I really believed that it was true—at least I really wanted it to be true. My mom always consoled me and told me that words could not harm me. Unfortunately, words do hurt. They can hit us harder than a fist at times. Words hurt us emotionally and this can be a greater pain to bear than a physical one. Think about the power of such phrases as:

- You are fat and lazy; you will never amount to anything.
- You always spill your milk, you klutz.
- Your room is always messy; you live like a pig.
- You never do anything right; you are worthless.

This is the kind of language that millions of children hear every day. After a while they start to believe it. What child is going to disagree with an adult? This kind of talk is a powerful form of programming that is difficult to overcome. Remember, most young people receive far more negative talk than positive. Therefore, it is critical that we understand the power of words and the physical and emotional impact they can have on other people.

Words can help or they can hurt, but they always have an impact. Henry Wadsworth Longfellow spoke to the depth of this problem when he said, "A torn jacket is soon mended, but hard words bruise the heart of a child." Regrettably, far too many people experience hurtful, limiting, degrading words that further cause them to lower their self-esteem and think poorly about themselves. It does not have to be this way, so how does this happen?

We Are Born to Win, But Programmed to Lose

I will always remember the words of motivational speaker, Dr. Alan Zimmerman, who said, "We are born to win, but programmed to lose." This powerful statement explains why words play such an important role in our early growth and development. The programming that we receive as children is a combination of words, thoughts, images, and experiences. These inputs provide the programming that determines who we are and what we value and believe.

As we learned earlier, language is a big part of our early development. The words that come from our parents, teachers, siblings, and friends are powerful because of the meaning we attach to them. Unfortunately, children do not have a lot of filters to protect themselves from negative words.

The problems identified by the researchers cited in the beginning of the chapter result from the fact that most adults do not understand the power of words. To make matters worse, millions of people don't know how to use them to bring out their best and the best in others. The negative programming that most children receive comes from parents who have no training or understanding about the powerful effects of words and affirmations. This results in millions of children being conditioned to lose when they are really equipped to win big in the game of life.

Claude Bristol, author of *The Magic of Believing*, thought that life is really all about suggestions. He believed that people are constantly accepting or rejecting each idea and experience that comes to them on a minute-by-minute basis. Some of the strongest programs that we develop (for good or for bad) are based on the words and suggestions of others.

The suggestions and programming that we receive as children determine how we think and act as adults. The way that we talk to ourselves and others reflects these programs. Self-talk is crucial to our ability to develop Say Power and use our words to bring out our best. Let us find out more about self-talk and how we talk to ourselves.

The Importance of Explanatory Style

Dr. Martin E. P. Seligman is an internationally known psychologist who has studied optimism, pessimism, and depression for over forty years. He devoted most of his adult life to the prevention of depression and helplessness in people, especially young people. Dr. Seligman developed programs that teach people how to increase their optimism and expand the degree of personal control that they have in their lives. One of Dr. Seligman's most significant findings was his discovery of the concept of "explanatory style."

Explanatory style is the way a person habitually explains how and why events happen. According to Dr. Seligman, the way a person describes what is happening in his or her life is a strong indicator of whether they feel like a helpless victim or whether they feel that they are in control of their life. It is also a reflection of whether a person tends to think about life in an optimistic or pessimistic manner. In his book, *Learned Optimism*, Dr. Seligman describes the three dimensions of explanatory style. He refers to them as the "three Ps" of explanatory style: Permanence, Pervasiveness, and Personalization. Let's look at each one and see how they relate to Say Power.

1. Permanence. Dr. Seligman believes that the dimension of permanence defines the duration of bad and good events in a person's life. Whether a person feels that events and circumstances are permanent or temporary is critical to the way that individual views and describes his or her life. Optimistic people are more likely to view setbacks and disappointments as temporary events. Pessimists, however, believe that difficult times are a permanent part of their disappointing existence. Optimists explain good events in a similar manner by expecting good events to happen while a pessimist thinks that luck is the only way anything good ever happens to them (Seligman, Pages 44-45).

2. Pervasiveness. The second part of explanatory style addresses the overall scope of events and circumstances. This dimension reveals how well a person can isolate negative events or whether they see bad events as catastrophic and all encompassing. For example, when a pessimist student fails a big test, he will probably say something like, "I'm a failure. I'll never pass this class." When an optimist fails an important test, she is more likely to say, "I failed the test, but I'll do better next time." The critical difference here is whether a negative event is viewed as having a universal impact on a person's life or whether it is limited to a specific event. There is a huge difference between failing a test and being a failure. (Seligman, Pages 46-47)

3. Personalization. The third part of the explanatory style concept looks at how much or how little ownership a person accepts for events and circumstances. Dr. Seligman's research indicates that when bad things happen, we always have two choices: we can blame our misfortune on ourselves or blame it on an outside source. The pessimist will blame him or herself for bad events and lower his or her level of self-esteem a notch or two when things do not go well. The optimist will blame other people or circumstances for the misfortune and maintain his or her self-esteem. Seligman's personalization dimension, the tension between internal and external forces, indicates whether a person is an optimist or a pessimist and whether they feel helpless or hopeful about life. (Seligman, Pages 49-50) Dr. Seligman's pioneering work validates the importance of our words and how we talk to ourselves. What we say about the events and circumstances in our life has a powerful impact on how we feel about ourselves, other people, and life in general.

What is Self-Talk and Why Is It Important?

Self-talk is a concept that is closely related to Dr. Seligman's work on explanatory style. Self-talk is the constant chatter that we carry on with ourselves every day. It is the habit of speaking to ourselves even while other people are speaking to us. Self-talk is usually done silently, but some of us do it out loud too. Our self-talk can be positive, or it can be negative. The important thing to remember is that we can control our self-talk and use it to bring out the best in ourselves and make the best out of what happens in our life.

Self-talk is important because it is the primary tool that we can use to overcome the negative programming that we received as children. Self-talk is crucial to our personal and professional success because it has a tremendous amount of control over our life. British diplomat, Benjamin Disraeli, once said, "Men govern with words." I have adapted his famous quote to say, "Men govern themselves and others with words." Words are powerful tools that leaders use to lead and inspire millions of people.

Our self-talk dialogue starts in the morning with the first words we think or say to ourselves as we get out of bed. Do you start your days off with something like, "Oh no, not another Monday, I want to go back to sleep." Or do you begin your days with empowering thoughts and words such as, "Wow, another Magnificent Monday. I know I am going to have another great day. I can't wait to get up and get moving." Which of these personal dialogues will help you live up to your potential and be the best that you can be? You have been programmed by all the thoughts and words that you have heard and said over the course of your lifetime. The good news is that you now have the power to change the way you talk to yourself.

Self-talk is another area where very few of us ever receive any formal training. Yet, the impact of what we say to ourselves can be devastating. Learning about the process of self-talk and how we talk to ourselves is one of the most important aspects of this book.

How Do You Talk to Yourself?

"How do you talk to yourself?" is one of the most important questions that you could ever think about. When you discover how you really talk to yourself day-in and day-out, you will discover the key to your current level of personal and professional success.

The research work conducted by Dr. Shad Helmstetter and other behavioral psychologists, shows that there are direct links between the way we talk to ourselves and the way we live. I have a saying that goes like this: "If you say you can or if you say you can't, you're absolutely right." The way we talk to ourselves is the way we are going to live. There really is a direct relationship between what we say and what we do. That is how powerful words are in our life.

One of the most powerful things that you can do for your personal development is to take a self-talk audit. Simply write down the personal conversations that you have with yourself for one day. They can be things that you say to yourself silently or out loud. At the end of the day, you will be amazed to discover how you really talk to yourself. You will be able to see trends in your self-talk. They may be positive, or they may be negative, but they give you a good indication about how you use one of the most powerful tools known to mankind—your words!

The Power of Affirmations

The power of self-talk is hidden in the patterns that we use to talk to ourselves. The patterns that we use to speak to ourselves are called affirmations. An affirmation is a declarative statement of fact or belief. The power of affirmations rests in two things. First, they are declared firmly and assertively. Second, they are either true, or believed to be true, by the person making them.

For example, a child who has been told that he is a good athlete for the first ten years of his life might affirm to himself, "I am a good basketball player." Another child of the same age could affirm, "I am a loser. I can't play sports" because of some negative experiences with the sport.

Both affirmations are powerful statements that have dramatically different impacts on each of the children. The first one could be both factual and believable. If a child has been told that he is a good athlete on a repetitive basis, then he is likely to believe it to be true. Compare this to the second affirmation where there is a factual discrepancy coupled with a false belief. The child is not a loser because he is not adept at sports. Unfortunately, if that's what the child believes, then it becomes a truth in that child's mind.

The real power of an affirmation comes from two sources. The first source is belief and the second is repetition. The dynamics of these two factors combine to make a powerful impact on the subconscious mind. Remember, the subconscious mind does not censor, it only processes information and drives us toward our predominant thoughts, words, and goals.

When the repetition is combined with the subconscious mind, it can have a powerful impact on self-image and personal performance. Our words serve as magnets that draw us to the future that we create with our mouth.

How Affirmations Work

Affirmations work because they serve as activators that your subconscious mind needs to start taking you toward your dreams and goals. Affirmations plant the instructions that your subconscious mind needs to re-program itself and achieve desired changes. After you begin this process, it adds greater awareness, focus, and direction to your life. Your subconscious mind starts to attract the behaviors and achievements that your affirmations describe.

Once you start consciously using affirmations, you will start seeing things that you have never seen before. You will experience greater focus and concentration in your life because your subconscious mind is leading you in the direction that you want to go. Finally, you will start moving closer to your goals and dreams each time you repeat your affirmations. Remember the subconscious mind does not censor, it only acts on what we tell it to act on. You can use affirmations to re-program yourself in ways that will help you become achieve any goal that you set. They can be educational goals, fitness goal, financial goals, or relationship goals. You have the power to become the wealthiest and most successful person that you can be.

How to Write Powerful Affirmations

Affirmations have a powerful impact on our self-esteem, our confidence, and our ability to accomplish almost every task. The question is, "Do your affirmations help you bring out your best or your worst?" Here are some same sample affirmations. Look at the different impact of affirmations that reflect powerless talk versus powerful talk.

Powerless Affirmations	Powerful Affirmations
I'm a failure.	I'm a winner.
I always goof things up.	I always learn from my mistakes.
I was just lucky.	I planned well and worked hard.
I'm too old to do that	I have the experience to do it.
I really blew it.	Next time, I'll get it right.

Empowering affirmations are excellent tools that can help you get the best out of your words and your self-talk. Learning how to increase your powerful affirmations and decrease your destructive affirmations is one of the best things you can ever accomplish in your life. Positive affirmations have the power to help you be and do your best. We can learn how to write affirmations that will keep us focused on becoming our best self. Here are some guidelines for writing powerful, positive affirmations:

1. Personal Focus. Include the letter "I" in every affirmation that you write. This provides the important link between what you want and your subconscious mind. Begin your affirmations with such phrases as *I am, I have, I love, I exercise, I own,* and *I weigh*. Or you can include "I" in the middle of an affirmation. One of the greatest affirmations ever written was by Frenchman Emile Coue: "Every day, in every way, I am getting better and better."

2. Positive Direction. State your affirmations in positive terms. Use words and expressions that attract you to your goal and avoid phrases that take you away from your desired performance. If you want to stop smoking, try, "I enjoy smoke-free living as of January 1, 2023." instead of saying "I am going to quit smoking." Or say, "Remember your lunch" instead of the usual "Don't forget your lunch." Your affirmations and your subconscious mind will pull you toward your goals and dreams. Teach yourself to focus on what you want and you will get what you want. That is how it works!

3. Present Tense. Write your affirmations as if you already own the behavior or habit that you want to acquire. Once again, this is the most powerful way to impact the subconscious mind. Affirmations that are stated in the present tense provide a direct link between your goals and your subconscious mind. This approach is based on the principle of *acting as if* you possess the behavior trait or goal that you desire. The strength of this method lies in the fact that directions given in the present tense are assumed to be true by the subconscious mind. The subconscious does not take time to argue with your commands and directions; it just works perfectly to make them part of your life.

4. Positive Emotions. You can increase the effectiveness of your affirmations by adding feeling words. Words like *love, enjoy,* and *passion* can provide a powerful link between your affirmations and your emotions. Remember, your subconscious mind cannot tell the difference between reality and a vividly imagined event or circumstance. Words that touch your emotions intensify the effect of your affirmations on your subconscious mind.

5. Possible or Realistic. Many of the world's greatest dreams had a lot of impossible in them. There is a fine line between what is possible and what is realistic. If you are sixty years old, it is pretty unrealistic to affirm to yourself that "I am in great shape and I will run a mile in five minutes or less." There are only a few people in the world who can achieve this feat. If you are not a world class runner, it is not possible or realistic to build this false hope. A better affirmation might be, "I take great care of myself by exercising daily and eating properly." Ultimately, you must be the judge of what you dream and affirm.

6. Focused and Specific. There is a place for general affirmations, but the more focus you have in your affirmations, the more powerful they will be. If you want to become a more confident speaker, affirm: "I am a confident speaker" instead of "I am improving my speaking ability." Any positive affirmation will help you program yourself for success and achievement. However, the more focused and specific your affirmations are, the more powerful they will be!

Secrets of Say Power

The next part of this chapter will explore some additional insights into the concepts of Say Power. These ideas will give you a greater understanding of the importance of Say Power and how you can use it to bring out the best in yourself and make the best out of what happens in your life. All these ideas are included to help you create an acute awareness of words and the critical role they play in your life and the lives of our loved ones and friends.

Secret # 1
Repetition is the key to Say Power.

The advertising industry knows this powerful secret. Now, so do you! Repetition plays a critical role in the reinforcement of any idea or advertising theme. Advertisers know that human behavior is largely determined by the words people hear and use, and the meaning and feeling that they attach to the words. We think in words and communicate in words.

The words that have the greatest impact on our lives are the ones that are repeated over and over. Therefore, companies invest millions of dollars to develop advertising campaigns. They know that words can have a powerful impact on people. We remember the jingles and advertising slogans because of the power of words and repetition. Most advertising campaigns are carefully planned to cause people to do something that will benefit the company that pays for the advertising. Buying a car, going to watch a new movie, or purchasing certain brand of athletic shoes are actions that companies want people to take because of paid advertising programs. The power of repetition is critical to the strategic plans of these businesses.

The results of a carefully planned advertising campaign can result in huge profits. Nike developed a simple slogan that contained only three words. The famous "Just Do It" mantra became the foundation of their print and media ads for decades. It also resulted in billions of dollars in sales. Words can be enormously powerful when combined with the power of repetition. Any questions?

We use these same principles every day of our lives, but sometimes we use them in the wrong way. Very few people know how to consistently make their words work for their benefit. As we learned earlier in this chapter, much of the programming that we receive as children is negative and limiting in nature. Instead of causing us to act and move toward success, most of our early programs held us back and kept us from reaching our true potential. Yes, learning how to use our words is a skill that must be mastered. The sooner we learn how to use our words the better our life will be. The key is how we talk to ourselves day in and day out. Author Alice Potter observed that "In personal programming, the operative word is repetition."

Secret # 2

Be careful how you talk to yourself because what you say is what you get.

Have you ever heard of the self-fulfilling prophecy? We must be incredibly careful how we talk to ourselves because what we say to ourselves is almost always what we get. In October 2005, the Chicago White Sox were on the verge of winning a playoff game that would send them to the World Series for the first time in eighty years. A television report came out a few days later about a sixty-eight-year-old lady Chicago Cub fan who told some friends that "If them damn sox go to the World Series, it will be the death of me." Guess what, the White Sox did win the

World Series and the poor woman died a few days later! Was this a coincidence? I am not so sure because the subconscious mind is always listening and acting on what we say—believe it. You can check out an article about her demise for yourself on Sports Mockery. (*Cubs Fan Dies of White Sox Hatred* by Nate Dusek dated September 3, 2015)

The farmer who plants beans will grow beans. And a person who plants corn is foolish to expect a harvest of radishes. The human condition works in similar fashion. If we are told that we are losers and we believe it, then we will probably grow up to be losers. If we talk in negative terms about our life and put ourselves down, we will continue to experience that sort of a lifestyle. How could the result be anything different?

If you take time to really listen to yourself, you will discover why you are living the way you do. The words that you speak and hear help build the hours and days that become your existence. If you discover that you are more pessimistic than optimistic, do not be upset with yourself or your parents. I am certain that your parents did the best that they could and probably reared you the same way that they were. I doubt that they had the benefit of learning from Dr. Seligman's research.

Although growing up with pessimistic parents can have a strong influence on your explanatory style, it does not have to be a permanent condition. Dr. Seligman's work indicates that with training and practice, people can develop a more positive, more optimistic, explanatory style. What you say to yourself ultimately determines your destiny. The bottom line is this: you must learn to manage your mouth!

Secret # 3

Your personal and professional success is directly proportional to your ability to manage your self-talk

Verbal skills constitute each person's basis for personal power. Yes, our ability to manage our mouth is critical to our personal and professional success. Anyone who wants to bring out the best in themselves and other people must learn how to use the power of words. People who understand the important role that words play in their lives will increase their personal success because their words will help them focus on their success—not other people.

Dr. Stephen Covey stated that "Our language, for example, is a very real indicator of the degree which we see ourselves as proactive people."(Covey, Page 78) Proactive people take responsibility for their life. They take responsibility for their thoughts, their words, and their actions. Their language reflects an understanding of the power of words and the important role they play. We can use our words to help ourselves and other people. Remember, it is always our choice. If we want to exert greater control over the way we think, act, and feel, we must take greater control over the way we talk to ourselves. That is the bottom line!

Secret #4

If you do not control your words and your programs somebody else will.

We have already learned the importance of programs in other parts of this book. As children, we had no control over our programs. However, as adults, we can control our programs and replace the ones that hold us back and keep us from being and doing our best. This is not an easy process, but it can be done through the power of affirmation and repetition.

Remember the mind is like a computer. It is only as good as the programs that run it, instruct it, and tell it what to do. GIGO is an expression in the computer world that means two different things. The first meaning is: Garbage In = Garbage Out. The second meaning is Good In = Good Out.

If we want to get good things out of our minds, we must put good things in. The thoughts and words that we experienced as children are responsible for the programs that we possess as adults. Everything we have thought, heard, and said has led us to this day. Every thought we think, hear, and speak will take us to our future.

All of us can take charge of our words and our lives. The sooner we take action to do this, the better we will be. We must be our own censors and we must be proactive in filtering out our negative thoughts and the negative thoughts of other people. We can be the programmers who can get it right. We can program ourselves to live the way we want to—the way that will help us become the best that we can be. If we do not use this opportunity, then other people will control our programs and our lives which is never good!

Secret #5

Use your subconscious mind to get positive results

If you want the subconscious mind to give you exactly what you want, you have to say exactly what you want. When my second son played varsity football, I had the privilege of working on the "chain gang" in a state championship semi-final football game. That meant I watched the game from the visitor's side of the field and helped to mark the location of the ball as it moved up and down the field. During the fourth quarter, the opposing team was moving down the field for the first score of a scoreless game. They were inside our team's twenty-five-yard line and a critical first down was only two yards away.

The opposing team's coach called a time out and brought his team to the sideline to discuss the upcoming play. He made sure everyone knew their assignments and sent his team back on the field.

One of the last players to leave the sideline was the halfback who would carry the ball on the critical play. As he trotted to the center of the field his coach said, "Don't fumble the ball."

Guess what the player did on the big play? Yes, he fumbled the ball. Ugh! I believe he fumbled the ball because the last three words he remembered were "Fumble the ball." I wonder what would have happened if his coach had said, "Hang on to the ball son, you're going to be a hero today?" I do not believe the coach wanted his player to fumble the ball, but that's exactly what happened. I do not believe that parents want their children to spill milk at the dinner table when they tell their children "Don't spill the milk." We cannot expect anyone to consistently achieve what we want them to achieve when we direct their focus to negative behaviors that we actually want them to avoid. We attract that which we think and talk about.

We cannot think bad and get good. It is impossible to talk in the negative and achieve the positive. We attract what we focus on. This is how the mind works and this is how life works. Instead of telling your child, "Don't forget your lunch" try something like, "Remember your lunch son." Why not say, "Be on time today" instead of saying, "Don't be late again"?

Secret # 6
Your self-talk does not have to be true to be powerful.

Our self-talk and our affirmations create powerful commands for our subconscious mind. Some of our strongest programs are often lies that have been repeated so often that they eventually sound like the truth. The story of Mr. Victor Serebriakoff, as told in Zig Ziglar's book *See You at the Top*, illustrates the power of programming. Victor was a man who had the intelligence of a genius.

Sadly, he grew up thinking that he was a dunce. As a child, Victor was told that he was a dunce for so many years, by so many different teachers and adults, that he had no choice but to believe what people said about him. Later, he learned that he was a genius when he took a test to become a skilled tradesman in the factory where he was employed. (Ziglar, Page 47)

This is a perfect example of a program that was not true, yet extremely powerful. Mr. Serebriakoff was a genius for most of his life, but he did not start acting like one until he acquired some new information (test results) and changed his beliefs. When he did this, he also had to start affirming that "I am a genius and I will live and work like a genius." Yes, the important question is this, "Are you in charge of your programs or is somebody else?"

The truth of our programs is never a consideration. A lie repeated often enough eventually sounds like the truth, but the truth repeated often enough will become reality. Words, by themselves, are neutral. What counts is the meaning that we attach to them. We can learn to attach meaning to the truth about ourselves and our potential instead of living lies from the past. Our self-talk and our programs can be used to bring out our best when done in a positive manner. Find the courage to program yourself the way you want to be programmed.

Secret # 7

People with Say Power know how to put their words and the words of others in perspective.

If you listen to people talk about themselves, you will hear some amazing things. You might hear someone declare, "I am a failure" when the truth could be stated as "I failed the test."

Or "I am a loser" becomes the most damaging way to explain that "I lost the game." People who are not aware of the powerful impact of their words don't understand the importance of putting their words in perspective.

The key to Say Power is learning to turn your self-talk into power talk by using words and affirmations that allow your subconscious mind to bring out your best self and the best in other people. The easiest way to do this is to decrease the emphasis on the negative affirmations and self-talk that you grew up with. Instead, learn to put more emphasis on the positive affirmations and self-talk that can help you create the future you desire. This process occurs gradually—one thought, one word, and one sentence at a time. That is how you were programmed to this point in your life and that is how you will change your programs.

Dr. Smiley Blanton offered some excellent advice when he said, "To be happy, drop the words "if only" and substitute the words "next time." This approach captures the essence of putting our thoughts and our words into perspective. When we dwell on our mistakes and reinforce the negatives in our life, we are adding power to the affirmations that we send to our subconscious mind. Dr. Blanton's approach is different. Instead of focusing on the mistakes of the past, he has given us a tool to detach ourselves from our shortcomings and focus our attention on improved performance.

I created a simple technique that builds on Dr. Blanton's idea. I call it "Instant Re-Say." Instant Re-Say is a powerful technique that can help you be more positive about the words you use. Whenever you catch yourself saying something negative, you simply re-state the negative phrase or affirmation in a positive way.

By focusing on next time, we are devaluing something that will do us no good and shifting our attention to the future—something that we still have a chance to control. With Instant Re-say, negative words and phrases can become power talk that will help you program yourself for success.

Here are some examples:

<u>Negative Phrase:</u> I really goofed up that sales call today.
<u>Instant Re-Say:</u> Next time, I will be totally prepared and make the sale.
<u>Negative Phrase:</u> I was too hard on John this morning.
<u>Instant Re-Say:</u> Next time, I will handle it better.

How to Increase Your Say Power

Here are twelve actions that will help you increase your Say Power and put power talk to work in your life. You have the power to reprogram yourself want. It will happen one thought and one word at a time. Use these ideas to develop scripts that will help you write and live the greatest life of all—a life of choice. Remember, work on your words and they will work on you.

1. **Conduct a self-talk audit.** Do a self-talk audit for at least one day and for an entire week if you really want to get the greatest benefit. The easiest way to do this is to carry a hand-held recorder and record as many of your words as possible. Then, take the time to

listen to the words that came out of your mouth. You will discover some powerful information when you go back and listen to your self-talk. Do your words and expressions bring out the best in yourself and other people? Or does it stop you before you even get started? Is your language full of optimism, or gloom and doom?

Do you regularly blame others for your circumstances or accept responsibility for your choices and your actions? The key to making the best use of your thoughts and words is the self-talk audit. Invest the time to discover how you talk to yourself. It will be one of the most beneficial personal development exercises that you can ever do. Good Luck!

2. Start every day with a positive phrase! Dr. Emile Coue's famous affirmation is a perfect way to start the day. Greet each day with "Every day, in every way, I am getting better and better." Zig Ziglar's phrase, "I'm super good and I'll get better" is also a great way to start any day. I usually begin my day with a special phrase that I have tailored for each day of the week. For instance, on Mondays I wake up and say something like: "Thank you for this Magnificent Monday Lord, I will use the talents you have given me to make the best of the next twenty-four hours."

I modify this phrase slightly for the rest of the week like this:
- Tuesdays are Terrific Tuesdays
- Wednesdays are Wonderful Wednesdays
- Thursdays are Tremendous Thursdays
- Fridays are Fantastic Fridays
- Saturdays are Spectacular Saturdays
- Sundays are always Super Sundays! (Not just once a year!)

3. Use the instant re-say technique to program yourself in a positive way. This is a powerful way to exercise positive control over your thoughts and actions. Instead of beating yourself up for making a mistake, transition yourself away from the mistake and focus on what you want to happen the next time.

If you can learn to place less importance on your mistakes and shortcomings and more focus on better performance, you are on your way to becoming your best self. Think about which approach is going to help you be and do your best. Is it "I'm so stupid—I messed up another speech" or "Next time, I will improve my outline and practice my speech at least five times."

4. Develop a series of power cards that contain your favorite affirmations. Organize your cards by topics such as attitude, self-image, health, fitness, faith, family, education, and career. Use some of your favorite affirmations that you have read or create your own. Write them on 3 x 5 cards and carry them with you. Or write them as "Notes" in your Smart Phone. When you have a few minutes at the start of the day, or during a break at work, read them. You can also read these cards when you are standing in line at the grocery store or waiting for a doctor's appointment. Instead of wasting your time, you can be programming your subconscious mind for greater success. If you are alone, read them out loud with passion! Remember, the truth repeated often enough eventually becomes reality.

5. Create power signs and put them where they will remind you to think and talk in powerful words and phrases. Use index cards and put them in places where you will see them during the day. Place your favorite affirmations on your dresser, nightstand, bathroom mirror, desktop, and your car dashboard. When you see the cards, repeat the affirmation out loud at least five times. This is a powerful technique that will help keep you thinking and talking in ways that will help you bring out the best in yourself and others.

6. Create your own power tape or compact disc." Create your own power notes on your I-Phone or Android device. You can also burn a CD of your favorite affirmations.

Alice Potter, author of *The Positive Thinker*, believed in the power of the spoken word and its ability to impact the subconscious mind. Potter claimed that the most familiar voice in our life is our own. A personal recording of your favorite affirmations is a powerful way to program the subconscious mind. Positive affirmations that are repeated frequently play a critical role in helping you program yourself for greater personal and professional success. Listen to your recordings in the morning when you are getting ready for the day or when you are driving to or from work. A power tape or power compact disc can help you turn idle time into power time.

7. Develop the habit of saying things in a positive manner. It is critically important that you use your words to focus on what you want for yourself and other people. Remember the best way to attract what you want for yourself and others is to say what you want, instead of what you do not want. Think about how you can eliminate the "Don't fumble the ball" and the "Don't spill the milk" expressions in your life. Tell yourself and others to "Hang onto the ball" and "Be careful with your glass." You can use the power of words and your subconscious mind to be the best that you can be. Wow—what a powerful way to talk and live!

8. Become a student of words and language. I urge you to read more about the power of words and increase your knowledge about this important life skill. Study the works of Dr. Shad Helmstetter, Alice Potter, and Dr. David Stoop. They have done extensive work in self-talk and affirmations. Their ideas on these subjects will help you turn your self-talk into power talk.

9. Write yourself power notes. Write yourself a power note when you want to remember something. When I lose track of a tool or a document, I write myself a power note that says something like, "Find the hammer" or "Find the Toastmaster file." I read this phrase out loud five times to plant the affirmation firmly in my subconscious mind and put the note on my bedroom dresser. I continue to read the card and repeat the affirmation until I find the missing item. This technique has only failed me once in thirty-years! It allows me to find what I am looking for. It also ensures that I spend zero time fretting and worrying about things that I misplace.

10. Eliminate "I Can't" from Your Vocabulary! I believe that the most destructive phrase in the universe is "I can't." These two words have stopped millions of people from being and doing great things. In fact, they stop most people before they ever get started. They hold people back; they build fear and cast doubt in the minds of too many people. The power that these two words possess is incredible. One of the most important decisions you can ever make is this: STOP USING THE WORD *CAN'T*—starting now!

In my opinion, the word "can't" is responsible for more wasted human effort and potential than any single word in the English language. Think about it! How many times have you said to yourself, "I can't do this" or "I can't do that"? Negative phrases like this affirm the worst in yourself and keep you from achieving goals that you have the ability and the power to achieve. I confronted this nasty little word over thirty years ago when I decided that I had had enough of this word! I examined the concept of "I can't" and discovered that it was really another way of saying two different things. It means that "I don't want to do something" or "I don't know how to do something."

Honestly, doesn't that cover most of the "I can't" situations? Yes, there are situations where physical disabilities absolutely prevent a person from doing certain things and "can't" becomes the real reason some people are not able to do some things. However, for most of us, "can't" is an excuse and not a reason for our lack of accomplishment. You can really take control of your thoughts and your words by making "I can't" disappear from your vocabulary. Take away the destructive power of these two words and replace them with positive phrases that express the choices and the decisions that you make about your abilities and your interests.

11. Conduct frequent vocabulary checks. Become acutely aware of the words you use. Take every word in your arsenal of speech as seriously as you can. Learn to distinguish between the words that weaken you and hold you back and the ones that empower you and help you be and do your best.

Look at the words below and start developing lists of your own. Whenever you find yourself using words that bring you down or take you away from your goals, substitute a more powerful word that will help you focus on being and doing your best.

Negative Words	Positive Words
Deadline	Target date
Failure	Experiment that didn't work
Obstacle	Opportunity
Problem	Challenge
Roadblock	Building block
Setback	Stepping stone
Weakness	Undeveloped strength

12. Make sure your words are at their best when things are at their worst. The absolute best time to come up with the right words is when things are going badly. Crisis situations and stressful events can reveal our best or our worst. The wrong word at the wrong time can destroy relationships, teams, and entire organizations. The adage "Silence is golden" is still good advice to follow in difficult situations. However, if you must say something, think before you speak and try to come up with words that will help you make the best out of a bad situation.

CHAPTER 5

CHOOSE TO MAKE TIME COUNT

> *It takes time to be a success, but all it takes is time.*
> —**Unknown**

We get twenty-four hours a day to do just about anything we want to do in life. However, if we do not use the precious seconds and minutes that we are given, they are gone forever. The key to achieving our personal, professional, and financial goals is time. If we choose to make our time count, we can live the best life of all—a life of choice. Unfortunately, if we do not make our time count, our lives won't count for much either.

Roman philosopher Laertius Diogenes stated that "Time is the most valuable thing a man can spend." After oxygen and food, nothing else is as important as time. It is the very essence of life. Time is something that we must understand and respect if we are to become our best selves. The purpose of this chapter is to remind you of the vital role that time plays in your personal and professional success. It is the resource that allows you to manifest your vision, your dreams, and your goals. Hour Power is the primary resource that we must invest to be and do our best.

Hour Power is the fifth topic of this book and certainly one of the most important. It is the habit of investing time in the dreams, goals, and actions that bring out the best in yourself and make the best of your time on earth. It is a way of living that focuses on life management instead of time management. It is the process of making wise choices about your time and your life. Hour Power is a way of living that says, "I am in charge of my choices and I am in charge of my life." It is a constant awareness of the value of time and the importance of using this valuable resource to create your best life. Finally, it is the ability to get the right things done at the right time, in the right way!

Why is Hour Power So Important?

The most valuable things in the world are normally things that are in short supply or things that cannot be replaced. Time is unique because there is plenty of it, but once it has passed, it is gone forever. American statesman John Randolph demonstrated a keen understanding of time when he said, "Time is at once the most valuable and the most perishable of all our possessions."

Time, and how we use it, is a critical part of the Choose and Grow Rich mindset. It is the framework that will be used to examine the concept of time and how it can help us be and do our best. Time is like water—it is so plentiful that it is often taken for granted. One of my favorite Irish sayings states it perfectly, "When God made time, He made plenty of it." It seems that there is always plenty of time, but this is a trap that is easy to fall into. If we treat time in a casual manner, it will drip away quietly, along with many of our hopes and dreams.

One of the most powerful thoughts I ever read about time is written below:

> I have been given this day to use as I will.
> I can waste it or use it for good.
> What I choose to do is important because
> I am exchanging a day of my life for it.

I do not know who wrote these words, but I have great respect for the wisdom they contain. If you believe that life has value, then you must also believe in the value of time. Everything that you do, or do not do, is divided into segments and it is in these segments that we live our lives. Hour Power is the key to getting the most out of your time and your life.

Benjamin Franklin understood that time was one of life's core issues. His famous comment about time is, "Dost thou love life? Then do not squander time, for that is the stuff life is made of." Mr. Franklin had great respect for the value of time. Time is a resource that we will always have in great supply and yet we always want more. We can spend our time on anything we want to, but we can only spend it once.

A Closer Look at Hour Power

I will discuss several different time issues that will help you think about time as a resource and the integral part it plays in your life. First, I will look at the factual side of time and help you determine the value of your time. Second, I will discuss some of the "time myths" that are popular today and assess their impact on your personal productivity and your level of Hour Power. Third, I will examine the "Top Time Thieves" that rob you of your time. Finally, I will explain the six keys that form the foundation of the Hour Power mindset.

Some Facts About Time

I went to the local post office in December 1999 and was intrigued by the digital millennium clock that was counting-down the exact number of days, hours, minutes, and seconds remaining in the calendar year and the twentieth millennium. The time on the clock was literally flashing by and there was nothing that anyone could do to stop it. This unique timing tool gave new meaning to the concept of how time flies. It caused me to be much more aware of the true nature of time because it was in a countdown mode. We knew that the end of the 20th century was approaching and there was nothing we could do to stop it. All we could do was make the absolute best of each minute, each hour, and each day that remained. I wonder how differently we would live if we knew exactly how many days we had left to live before we died? Would we make better use of this precious resource if we knew how far we had come in our life and how far we had to go?

Here are some facts that I learned, or relearned, about time as I researched and wrote this chapter:

- Time is a valuable resource
- Time is a system of measurement
- Time is allocated in organized units
- Some of our time is controlled by other people
- Every unit of time is only as valuable as we make it

Everything we ever hope to do in life requires time—everything! It is absolutely the most valuable resource with which to build a successful life. Most of us have far more time available to us than we ever use effectively.

Here are some facts about time that should give you a greater appreciation for the incredible amount of time that is available to us every year.

- The number of seconds in a minute = 60
- The number of seconds in an hour = 3,600
- The number of seconds in a day = 86,400
- The number of seconds in a week = 604,800
- The number of seconds in a month = 2,592,000
- The number of seconds in a year = 31,536,000

- The number of minutes in an hour = 60
- The number of minutes in a day = 1,440
- The number of minutes in a week = 10,080
- The number of minutes in a month = 43,200
- The number of minutes in a year = 525,699

- The number of hours in a day = 24
- The number of hours in a week = 168
- The number of hours in a month = 720
- The number of hours in a year = 8,760

It is hard to imagine that anyone would ever complain about not having enough time. Everyone has plenty of seconds, minutes, and hours to accomplish their most cherished dreams and goals.

And yet, one of the biggest complaints that people make is that they never have enough time to do what they want. Again, the problem is not how much time you have or do not have, but how you choose to use it. The choices we make determine the ultimate value of our time and our life.

What is Your Time Worth?

The chart below illustrates the value of an hour's work. These numbers are based on a forty-five-hour work week and a forty-nine weeks work year. This works out to 2,205 work hours or 132,300 work minutes. Take a look at what your work time is worth.

Income Level	Minute Value	Hourly Value
$15,000.00	11.3 cents	$6.80
$20,000.00	15.1 cents	$9.07
$25,000.00	18.9 cents	$11.33
$30,000.00	22.7 cents	$13.61
$40,000.00	30.2 cents	$18.14
$50,000.00	37.8 cents	$22.67
$75,000.00	56.0 cents	$34.01
$100,000.00	75.6 cents	$45.35
$250,000.00	$1.88	$113.37
$500,000.00	$3.78	$226.75
$1,000,000.00	$7.55	$453.51

Yes, time is a precious resource that should never be taken for granted. When I first examined a chart like this, I developed a greater respect for my time and the value I placed on it. Time, unlike money, cannot be saved for a rainy day. The most important questions about time are:

- What is your time worth?
- How do you spend your time?
- How will you use time to achieve your goals?
- What is the most important thing that you could be doing right now?

If you take the time to ask yourself these questions and really think about the answers, you will discover some important information that is vital to your future success. This simple chart led me to the conclusion that you can spend your time and your life on anything you want, but you can only spend it once.

A Closer Look at Seven Time Myths

Hundreds of books have been written about time. It is one of the most popular topics in the publishing industry. I have read many of these books because they promised things that I wanted to learn about time. Unfortunately, too many "time" books promise things that they cannot deliver. In fact, some of them spread myths about time that are simply not true. Here are seven myths about time that I have identified in the popular literature on this important subject.

1. Time can be managed. There are many books in bookstores and on library shelves that promise to teach you the skills of time management and improve your ability to manage time. Do you really believe that time can be managed? You will have more success managing your dog or cat if you approach time as something to be managed. The simple truth is that time manages fine without us. Nobody really manages time, but we can all manage ourselves and our choices about how we use the time we have each day.

2. Time can be saved. Have you heard the claims by time management experts that they can teach you how to save time? Have you ever saved time? Where did you put your savings? Did you put them in a savings account or a mutual fund? Yes, I know I am playing word games here, but this is an important concept that affects our attitude about time and how we can get the most out of every hour and every day.

We can never save time, but we can plan better, organize better, and use our time more effectively. Ultimately, our choices about time give us more time to invest in projects and activities that will help us to be and do our best.

3. Time can be mastered. Have you seen the seminars and book titles that promise to teach people how to master time? Once again, people do not master time; time is its own master. It is not something that can be mastered like a language or a musical instrument. Time is a precious resource that can only be used or wasted. The best that we can do is learn to master ourselves which can lead to better choices and decisions about how we use the hours, minutes, and seconds of our life.

4. Time can be organized. Another popular myth about time is that we can be taught how to organize it better. Folks, I am here to tell you that time is already organized. It is divided into uniform segments according to seconds, minutes, hours, days, weeks, years, decades, and centuries. Yes, time is already very well organized! We should spend less time trying to organize our time and more time organizing ourselves. Calendars, computers, and telephone apps are wonderful tools that can help us make the most of our time.

5. Time can be controlled. Believe it, or not, there are time management authorities that promise to teach us how to control our time. Do not believe this myth either because nobody controls time. Time has a pattern and a rhythm that cannot be controlled. There is not a human being on earth who can stop it, start it, slow it down, or speed it up. Time is always there, in one-second increments and there is nothing we can do to affect it any way. We simply make choices about how we will use the time available. Fortunately, that is all the control we need to achieve our dreams and goals.

6. Time can be maximized or increased. Have you ever heard someone say that he or she found a way to maximize their productivity at work or increase their free time? Of course, this too, is impossible to do. People who talk like this want to find a way to add seconds, minutes, and hours to each day in hopes that they can somehow get seventy-five seconds out of a minute or maybe thirty-six hours out of each day. Once again, time cannot be expanded or changed in any way. Any maximizing or increasing in this area must come from changes we make in how we value and use this priceless resource. It is just that simple.

7. You can learn to find more time. Some time management experts claim that after you spend money on their seminar or book, you will be able to find more time to do the things you really want to do in life. I often wonder where they tell you to look for all this extra time. Is it hidden in the closet, or under your desk at work, or in the back of your personal organizer? Unfortunately, the bad news is that more time cannot be found. However, the good news is that we can learn to make better choices about how we use our time and how well we align our actions with the goals and dreams we have established in our life. I recommend that if you do want to go looking for more time, go look in the mirror. The person who is your time problem and your time solution will be looking back at you. You cannot learn to find more time, but you can learn to respect time.

A Closer Look at the Worst Time Thieves

I was fortunate to teach an innovative high school program called The Successful Living Program. Our innovative curriculum taught important "life skills" like positive thinking, goal setting, problem solving and personal productivity skills. I always enjoyed the reactions of my adult students when we discussed the topic of "Time Thieves."

Here are the top time thieves mentioned in our discussions:

- Telephone interruptions
- Lack of objectives, priorities, and planning
- Attempting to do too much

- Drop in visitors at work and home
- Ineffective delegation
- Personal disorganization
- Inability to say "No"
- Procrastination

Yes, this was before the internet, email, and smart phones. So, there are even more "Time Thieves" in the Twenty First Century, aren't there? How many of these time wasters nibble away at your seconds, minutes, hours, and days? Everyone struggles with them at some point, right? And yet, just about all of them are habits or personal choices that we can control. This is incredibly good news because it means that we can change these behaviors and learn new habits that will help us increase our Hour Power.

Managing your choices and your actions in relation to time can help you reach your dreams and goals. Time is one of the most powerful resources that successful people use to be the best that they can be. At the end of this chapter, we will examine some techniques that you can use to eliminate these thieves from your life.

The Six Keys to Hour Power

My research and personal experience with Hour Power led me to the discovery of six fundamental secrets regarding the effective use of time.

These secrets provide the foundation for most of the time techniques described in time management literature. My six keys to Hour Power are listed below. I will explain each one in detail.

- Alignment
- Balance
- Choices
- Planning
- Priorities
- System

Alignment. Alignment is critical to our personal and professional success. It establishes the focus that we need to get the most out of our time and our life. There are four components to the alignment part of the Hour Power process. The first part is vision. If we have a personal vision for our lives, then we have a basic direction that brings us greater focus. The second part is mission. When we have a mission, we begin to live with much more focus and can make better choices about our time and our life. The third part is purpose. With purpose, we know what we are doing and why we are doing it. Finally, when we live by our values, we know what things fit in our life and what things do not.

When we align our vision, mission, purpose, and values; we will have less trouble making choices about time. We will know what is important and what's not important. Alignment is a powerful concept that greatly increases our productivity and personal power. Aligning the clock with what is important in your life helps you make better choices and decisions about time. This approach allows us to enjoy the benefits of synergy that truly enables us to make our time count. More importantly, it allows us to make our lives count!

Balance. Balance is especially important to us because it helps us keep our time and our life in perspective. As a young football coach, Dick Vermeil displayed a sign in his locker room that read, "The best way to kill time is to work it to death." Such an approach to coaching and life will throw anyone out of balance. In 1982 forty-two-year-old Vermeil retired from coaching because he was "burned out." Sadly, he was so obsessed with football that he was a miserable person. Vermeil said that he could not handle losing and didn't enjoy winning. He was a workaholic who had lost the balance in his life. Coach Vermeil's story reinforced the importance of time and balance. We cannot overwork ourselves and ignore our health, family, and peace of mind without developing problems. Balance is critical to our overall health and quality of life.

Choices. Ultimately, the choices that we make about time determine the quality and quantity of our life. The power of choice is the greatest power in the world. Yes, life is simply a series of choices that lead to desired results or undesirable consequences. We make hundreds of choices every day about time and how we use it. Legendary motivational guru Jim Rohn stated it perfectly: "Either you run the day, or the day runs you." People who choose to "run their day" are the ones who will live the best lives. Hopefully, you are, or will become, one of these people.

Planning. Planning is essential to learning how to get the most out of your time and your life. Consider the popular saying, "If you don't have time to do it right, when will you find the time to do it over?" Planning is a habit that can help us get the best out of ourselves and our time. It is estimated that eighty percent of the people do not think ahead more than a week or ten days. It is not surprising that they don't get the most out of their time or their life.

There is a critical connection between planning and our ability to effectively use time. Planning is a habit that pays big dividends in the challenge of adding "More power to each hour." A few minutes of planning at the beginning or end of each day is one of the best time investments we can make. Henry Kaiser expressed this idea perfectly when he said that "One minute of planning is worth two in execution." (More on planning in Chapter Six)

Priorities. The ability to establish priorities is vital. Unfortunately, most people fail to prioritize their daily activities on a regular basis. Yet, they are puzzled and wonder why they fail to achieve the personal and professional goals they profess to desire. Very few people have so much money that they do not have to budget and prioritize their spending. It is the same way with time. We must treat it as a limited resource even though we have more time than we will ever use effectively. Setting priorities is critical if we are to make the best use of our time and get the most out of each hour. When we know what is important to us, it is easier to put things in perspective. This is the key to getting the most out of our time and our life!

System. There are a large variety of personal organizers available today. The good news is that you only need one system—one that works for you! Yes, there are still paper-based systems and cell phone applications that can help you track your daily and week schedule plus a variety of other activities. It really does not matter what system you use as long as you choose one that you like. With the right tools, you can develop a systematic approach to planning your weekly and monthly activities. These tools can increase your personal productivity and enable you to accomplish more each day. Personally, I use a combination of a personal paper calendar system and my cell phone to schedule my day and achieve my goals.

The Secrets of Hour Power

Hour Power is a critical concept in the Choose and Grow Rich program because it is the single greatest resource that we have available to create the life we want to live. Now it is time to expand on some of the ideas that were introduced earlier in this chapter and add some new thoughts. Let us learn more about how we can make the best use of our time and increase our Hour Power.

Secret #1
Time is the great equalizer.
Everyone who lives a day gets the same deal.

Think about it. There is no other resource in the world that is distributed as fairly and as equitably as time. As people, we are all different in so many ways, but we are exactly alike when it comes to the distribution of time. There is absolutely no discrimination of any kind when it comes to time. Another one of my favorite quotes on time comes from the legendary Jim Rohn who said, "Time is more valuable than money. You can get more money, but you can't get more time."

Yes, time is absolutely the great equalizer. According to Mr. Rohn, not even a billionaire like Bill Gates can buy more time than you or me. We all get the same daily ration of twenty-four hours. I can use my hours any way that I want to. That is a lot of freedom, don't you think? It is also a great responsibility that we must take seriously if we are to live our best life and become the best person that we can become.

Time is one of the greatest examples of personal freedom in the universe. Most adults have almost unlimited control over the ways they use each second, each minute, each hour, and each day of their lives.

There is still much injustice in this world and many people are hindered by prejudice in blatant and subtle ways. Time, however, is one of the purest forms of personal expression on the planet. Yes, our boss or immediate supervisor may control more of our time than we like. Of course, family responsibilities can devour a large amount of our daily time allotment. Still, we have a great deal of freedom and control over the time we are given each day.

Time is the fundamental resource of life and it is the key to so many good things that we strive to achieve and enjoy. Those who know its secrets and its power are truly blessed and live with a peace of mind that is uncommon. Take time to think about the beauty of time and how it is the ultimate source of freedom and personal power. With time there are no "haves" and "have nots." Everybody has the same amount of time—not one second more or one second less. What makes the difference is how we use it. This amazing concept is as simple and as powerful as any idea in the universe.

Secret #2
If you do not take charge of your time somebody else will!

This is a law of life that ranks right up there with the law of gravity. Remember, a scientific law always works; it applies to everybody, whether they agree with it or not. Many people do not like the idea that other people can control their time, but it is a fact of life. Very few people are totally in control of all their time. However, we can control most of it.

Writer Carl Sandburg demonstrated a clear understanding of the importance of time when he wrote, "Time is the coin of your life…and only you can determine how it will be spent. Be careful lest you let other people spend it for you."

Time, like any valuable resource, is something that must be closely watched and carefully protected. The previous list of "Time Thieves" provided numerous examples of situations where other people gain control of our time if we let them. Again, if you do not have a plan for using your time, somebody else will! Has anyone ever asked you if you "Do you have five minutes to look at this project?" What usually happens is that the five-minute request turns into a twenty-to-thirty-minute interruption. If you do not take charge of your time, somebody else always will!

Guard your time carefully and invest it in actions and activities that will lead you to the successful achievement of your goals. Always be polite when dealing with interruptions and distractions. However, make it clear that you are in charge of your time. Always remember that no one can waste your time without your consent. Make it a habit to get more power out of each hour and you will be well on the way to making the most of your time and your life.

Secret #3

If you feel that you have a problem with time, remember that time is not the problem—you are!

Time is one of the most talked about and most written about topics in life. I have never heard anyone complain that they have too much time, but I have joined millions of others in my complaints about the lack of it. However, the more I learned about time, the more I understood that the real problem was not time, it was me! Now, I know the truth about time. Time is always there for me to use or misuse as I see fit. Ralph Waldo Emerson expressed it perfectly when he said, "This time, like all times, is a good one if we just know what to do with it." The real reasons we have trouble with time is because we have no goals, lose our focus, or just get lazy with our time.

The best way to confront your time problem is to look at the mirror, not at the clock. You cannot fix time, but you can fix you! The clock does not make you late and it doesn't schedule too many activities in one day, does it? You are the person who makes the plans, accepts the meetings, and tries to juggle ten glass balls at the same time. Golda Meier, former Prime Minister of Israel, understood the time problem perfectly. She said that "I must govern the clock, not be governed by it." Of course, we know that she did not govern the clock—no one can do that—but she learned to govern herself and a country too. Golda Meier knew that time, like life, is always what you make of it and she learned to make the best use of both.

Secret #4

You gain the most control in your life when you start controlling your choices about time.

You control your life by controlling your choices. Of course, many of your choices are about time. Charles Buxton gave us a great truth about time when he said that "You will never find time for anything. If you want time, you must make it." The way we make time for the things we want to be and do in life is through our choices. I have already expressed my feelings about the importance of choices in life, but I cannot over-emphasize this critical concept. Choice Power is our greatest power because it is the power that we use the most in life. Everything we do or do not do in life begins with a choice. You will see dramatic improvements in the quality of your life when you start making better choices about how you invest your time every day!

Yes, many of our choices are about time and how we decide to use this valuable resource every day. We make hundreds of choices about time in a single week. Time is a resource that can be invested wisely or squandered foolishly. Lost, or wasted, time can never be recovered—it is gone forever!

When you start to view time as a resource to be invested instead of a currency to be spent, you will start making better choices about what you do with your time. We show the world what we value by how we spend our time and how we spend our money. Show the world that you place the highest possible value on your time and make choices that demonstrate this belief. Use your greatest power to make the choices that will help you get the most out of your time, yourself, and your life.

Secret #5
Time does not cause stress, people do.

Yes, time plays a critical role in our life. It is the topic of more personal choices than any other single area of our life. Some people make a lot of good choices about their time and their life. They enjoy the benefits of these choices and one of the biggest benefits is reduced stress. However, other people make a lot of bad choices and they pay the price with a stress-filled life. Time is often blamed as the culprit that causes many of our problems.

If you think about it, time cannot make us happy or sad. Time is harmless. Time cannot affect us negatively unless we choose to let it happen. Time is neutral. It is incapable of affecting us in any way. What causes all the trouble is the attitude we have about this wonderful resource and the way we think about it. When you listen to people who are stressing about time, it does not take long to hear the truth.

What people are really saying is that they are choosing to think, talk, and act in ways that are counterproductive to their stated goals and responsibilities. Instead of looking at themselves and their lifestyle, most people prefer to blame time for their high stress levels, career frustrations, and reduced quality of life. Yes, time does get a bad rap!

The best solution to this problem is to examine our attitudes about time and how we spend and invest this valuable resource. Think about it: have you ever heard a baby complain that he or she does not have enough time or that my schedule is just too busy? Young children are born with a natural rhythm about life that is basic. As they grow older and become exposed to modern life, they learn about stressful living from the adults they grow up with. Stressful living is an acquired behavior that does not have to be a permanent part of your life. Take charge of your time and you will reduce the unnecessary stress in your life—I promise!

Secret #6
Our words do much to determine whether we view time as our ally or our enemy, as friend or foe.

The words and phrases we verbalize about time have a powerful impact on how we use or abuse this precious resource. We already learned about the importance of words in the chapter on Say Power. Remember, what we say is normally what we get. If you plant beans, it is pretty hard to harvest corn. The same is true with our words. What we say about time and how we say it determines how much we really get out of our time and our life. If you sit in an office, or a busy restaurant, for more than a few minutes you will likely hear people talking about time and the stress that it causes in their lives.

Have you ever heard expressions like, "I don't have enough time to finish this project" or "My schedule is killing me"? These statements illustrate the negative effects that people suffer from a lack of understanding of the true nature of time and the role it plays in their lives. If you really want to get more out of your time and your life, you must start with the basics. Make sure that your own words are not sabotaging your efforts.

Secret #7
The best question you can ever ask: What's Important Now?

I learned to ask the most powerful question you can ask yourself about time from former college football coach and television commentator Lou Holtz. The best way to get the most out of your time and your life is to frequently ask the WIN question. The letters in the word **WIN** make up the question "What's

Important Now?" I believe this simple question is one of the most powerful techniques available to get the most out of every second, minute, and hour of our life. Starting today, begin the habit of asking yourself the WIN question throughout the day. Asking the win question can do more to improve your choices about how you use your time than anything else you will read in any book on time management.

The answers to the WIN question will be easier when you know what your goals are and when you have determined what your priorities are in life. Your choices and decisions will be much clearer when you know what you want to accomplish each day, each week, and each month of your life. If you use the WIN question in conjunction with the other techniques in this book, you will put yourself in position to be a big winner in the game of life.

How to Increase Your Hour Power

So far, I have examined time and the concept of Hour Power in considerable detail. Now, I will look at some of the actions you can take to make more effective use of your time and increase your ability to get the right things done at the right time. Here are ten steps that you can take to develop your life management skills and increase your Hour Power. Remember, you do not have to try all these ideas at once. Instead, try them one at a time and you will find the ones that work best for you!

1. **Conduct a Personal Time Audit.** Before you can learn to increase your Hour Power, you must know how you currently use your time. A time audit is the first key to gaining greater control over your life and the choices you make about time. Use a time log to keep a record of your daily activities for at least seven consecutive days. This process will help you see how you spend your time. Be accurate and capture as many of the little things that eat up your time as possible.

2. Analyze Your Time Log. Once you have a week's worth of information you will be able to analyze your time-spending habits. A time log is a valuable tool that will help you discover the habits and actions that may be robbing you of valuable time. Your time log can help you find ways to eliminate unwanted or unnecessary activities and replace them with actions and activities that will help you get more power out of each hour. If you are true to this project, you will some valuable information that can help you be more productive in your personal and professional life.

3. Invest in a Personal Planner System. There are a wide variety of paper-based and electronic personal planner systems available in many price ranges. You do not need to spend a fortune to acquire one of these systems. A personal planner is an essential tool that can help you become a more focused and better organized person. The biggest advantage of a personal planner is that it helps you to align your mission, purpose, vision, and values with your goals and daily actions. Writing things down and having them in one place is also a great way to remember more and forget less. A planner allows you to schedule the events and actions that will get you where you want to be in life. We have outlined many of the rules of the time game in this chapter. Bottom line—a personal planner is an ally that will help you get the most out of your time and your life!

4. Develop Planning Routines. Planning is one of the best investments that you can make with your time. Even fifteen minutes of planning before the next day, or at the beginning of each week and month, can really help you increase your effectiveness. Developing a "planning habit" helps up stay organized and remain focused on what is most important to you. Most "time" experts recommend daily planning sessions of twenty to thirty minutes to look ahead and get organized for the next day. Some people do their best planning at the beginning of each day. Others like to finish each day by planning the next.

Personally, I like to plan for the next day just before I go to bed. The most important thing about daily planning is that you do it every day, at a time that works best for you. The same approach works very well for weekly and monthly planning. A thirty-minute investment of time at the beginning of each week or month will help you organize your activities and your actions. Planning is a great way to reduce your stress and increase your success.

5. Prioritize, Prioritize, Prioritize. Develop the habit of doing first things first. If you do not have any dreams or goals it doesn't really matter what you do with your time. But, if you do have dreams and goals, then time matters—a lot. The more you want to accomplish in life, the more you need to prioritize your actions and activities. The habit of prioritizing allows you to get the more power and productivity out of each hour. Prioritizing is such an important task that businessman Charles M. Schwab, then President of Bethlehem Steel, challenged a consultant named Ivy Lee to "Show me a way to get more things done. If it works, I'll pay anything within reason." (Mackenzie, Page 38) It took Lee about three months to train Schwab's managers in what is now known as the Ivy Lee Method.

Lee's method required managers to take fifteen minutes at the end of the workday to make a list of the six most important tasks to be done the next day. Then, each item on the list was to be prioritized. Mr. Lee trained the Bethlehem Steel managers to start working on the first item on their list and continue working until completion. Then, he told them to work on the next item and so on. Whatever remained undone at the end of the day was moved to the top of the next day's list unless something more important was added. Schwab's team implemented the idea and his company's productivity improved significantly. In fact, it improved so much that Schwab wrote a check to Mr. Lee for $25,000.00 for this valuable system. That same amount would be valued at $500,000.00 in 2023 dollars! Later, Mr. Schwab declared that "this was the most profitable lesson he ever learned in his entire business career." (Mackenzie, Page 39)

Yes, that bit of wisdom has stood the test of time. There really is no good reason not to begin each day with a clear focus on the next twenty-four hours. The Ivy Lee Method will help you do exactly that!

6. Turn *Down Time* into *Power Time*. Travel time, time spent waiting in line, or waiting for meetings or appointments is often considered down time for many people. Many people become frustrated and even angry when they are not properly prepared for these situations. You can turn this wasted time into power time by planning and developing the habit of getting more power out of each hour. If you spend a lot of time driving back and forth to work, listen to educational materials on compact discs or podcasts while you commute. There are thousands of books and self-improvement materials now available that can help you learn while you drive. Always have something to write with and something to write on as you go through the day. Finally, always have something to read while you are waiting for an appointment or interview. Wait time does not have to be wasted time! This powerful habit puts me in position to be productive even in the most stressful and frustrating situations. It will do the same for you!

7. Learn to say "No." This is one of the most important skills you can master in your effort to get the most out of your time and your life. Saying "No" is not that hard to do if you follow the other suggestions listed in this section. If you take the time to frequently review your vision, mission, purpose, values, and goals you will always know where you are headed. Saying "No" is always a choice between doing what will take you where you want to go and what will not. Sometimes, your "No" will mean that the timing for your involvement may not be right at the current time but could be in the future. In other cases, you simply may not want to invest any time in the activity or action that someone asks you to participate in. Learning to say "No"(nicely and firmly) is one of the best skills you can learn. It will help eliminate unwanted commitments and unnecessary stress from your life.

8. Be flexible and balanced about Your Time. The first thing I advise about using a paper-based personal planning is to make all entries in pencil. Change is inevitable, especially with your daily plans and schedule. If you think that a personal planner is going to make every day a perfect day—forget it! Perfection is impossible to attain, but excellence is possible. Develop the habit of under-scheduling whenever possible. This gives you built-in flexibility when unexpected events occur in your day. It will keep the stress level down to a more manageable level. You can also schedule blocks of time for routine activities like making phone calls, reading e-mail, and attending routine meetings. Of course, if you need an hour or two to work on a big project, then schedule it. Once you block your time, do not allow any interruptions except for emergencies!

9. Ask the WIN Question—A Lot! Again, one of the absolute most important habits you can develop is the habit of asking the WIN question. It is never a bad time to ask, "What's Important Now?" You can also practice the simple method used by multi-millionaire and philanthropist W. Clement Stone. He used the phrase "Do It Now" to build a fortune in the life insurance business and magazine publishing. The WIN question will help you discover the critical actions that you need to take at any one time so that you can do it now. When you combine the ability to know what you should be doing with the ability to act, you will develop a power that will allow you to consistently get the most out of your time, yourself, and your life!

10. Treat Time Like a Valuable Asset. Earlier in this chapter, we learned that all of us are millionaires when it comes to time. We are all wealthy if you measure the seconds, minutes, hours, and days that we have already used and will have available to use in the future.

When you think about it, we all have an unlimited supply of time to use or misuse as we choose. German philosopher Wolfgang Von Goethe revealed this secret hundreds of years ago when he said, "One always has enough time, if one will apply it well." If you believe that life has value, then you must also believe in the value of your time. Time, unlike money, cannot be saved for a rainy day. It is spent in one-second amounts that add up to the minutes, hours, and days of our lives. Money cannot buy yesterday, it can't buy more tomorrows, and it definitely can't buy more time!

Yes, time is simply a "use it or lose it" proposition. The important question is always, how do you spend and invest your time? You have the freedom to spend a day's time on anything you want, but you can only spend it once. Time is more likely to reward you with the results you want in life when you learn how to make your time count. Develop the habit of making the most of the time you have and you will be able to live a life that most people only dream about. Time can be your greatest ally in your quest to achieve personal success. It can also be your best friend, along with the power of compounding, in achieving wealth.

CHAPTER 6

CHOOSE TO PLAN

Most people don't plan to fail, they fail to plan.
—John L. Beckley

John L. Beckley's simple quote is a critical key to getting the best out of yourself and your life. Good advice does not get any better than these ten words. Yes, Mr. Beckley was a big believer in the power of planning and so am I! My term for the ability to plan your work and you are your plan is "How Power." A good plan is the way you connect your dreams and goals with what you need to do to achieve them. How Power is the habit of planning that allows people to accomplish the right goals at the right time. It is the ability to visualize an objective, create a plan, and follow that plan to the desired destination. It is a habit of thinking that says, "I know where I want to go and I have a plan to get there." How Power is the ability to ask yourself the right questions and think through potential problems that you may encounter in your quest to achieve your goals. It is a way of life that allows us to exercise the maximum amount of control over our destiny and create our desired future. Yes, a good plan, not a perfect plan, will help you get ready for your best life.

Yes, How Power is the best way to get ready for your best life—one that has an abundance of success, prosperity, and loving people to share it with! How Power helps you get ready for the life you are destined to lead. It gives you the ability to plan for your future on your terms. The following quote summarizes the importance of planning. "A plan is a trap that is set to capture the future." I do not know who authored this phrase, but I love the concept. The rest of this chapter is dedicated to teaching you how to develop plans that will help you capture your best life!

Why is How Power Important?

How Power is important because it provides the critical link between where we are and where we want to go. The important thing to remember is that goals provide the direction in our life and plans provide the path. One of my former mentors was a great believer in the power of planning. He told me that "Proper prior planning prevents poor performance." I believe that this concept applies to all aspects of our personal performance. All areas of our life require some sort of planning if we are to achieve our goals and become the best person that we can become.

How Power is an important element of successful performance and achievement in almost every profession and career field. Airline pilots cannot get permission to schedule a flight until they submit a detailed flight plan. Contractors cannot get a permit to build a house without a set of approved blueprints. An aspiring entrepreneur will not be able to attract investors without a sound business plan. Teachers are required to develop lesson plans to guide their instructional efforts. Football coaches develop game plans to produce victory on the athletic field. Movie directors follow a script that lays out every spoken word and scene in every movie that is produced.

Yes, planning is a major part of business and economic life and it should also be a big part of our personal life. It is a skill that can help us reach our goals and live the best life that we can live.

Aristotle once said, "Well begun is half done." A well-designed plan is the best way to begin any project. Unfortunately, planning is perceived to be hard work and is avoided by millions of people every day. When you think about it, most people spend more time preparing their grocery lists than they do planning their life.

However, if we look at planning as a wise investment of time, and effort, we will make time for this important activity. Plans can be simple or complex. They can be formal or informal. The important thing to remember is that any plan is always better than no plan.

Why Don't More People Use the Power of Planning?

Why don't more people use the power of planning? I used to ask my seminar students this question. The answers I received were like ones I received when I asked them why they failed to set goals. Here are some of the most common responses:

- I don't have time to plan
- I don't know how
- I tried it and it didn't work
- It is too hard
- I'm doing fine without planning, why should I change?

Do any of these reasons sound familiar? I have used them all and I am sure that you have also used some of these reasons, right? Like most people, I was not a big believer in planning until I joined the United States Army. That is when things changed for me!

To Plan or Not to Plan?

This is the big question that everyone faces every day. Remember, we have lots of choices to make in our lives and planning is another one to think about. We can choose to make life happen the way we want it to happen (or close to it) or we can wake up every morning and see what happens.

Living without planning is what I call the Plunge Ahead Method. People who plunge through life are usually busy. They do what appears to be the right things and they handle problems as they arise. Unfortunately, this method leads to a pattern of one crisis after another. People who live like this spend most of their time getting in and out of their difficulties and struggling to get ahead in life. Yes, Plunge Ahead people spend most of their life reacting to what happens instead of making their best life happen!

The other method of living is what I call the Plan Ahead Method. People who plan are more likely to be effective in their life and more in control of their personal destiny. They know where they want to go and they usually have some kind of a plan to get there. The planners take time to reflect, analyze, and consider alternatives about their future. They often avoid hasty judgments and crisis situations because they have direction. The best planners are also flexible. They can take advantage of opportunities that arise. Good planners are always alert for situations and people who can assist them with their goals and plans. In conclusion, people who plan ahead are more likely to get ahead because they know what they want and they go out and get it!

Bottom line—you don't have to become compulsive about planning. However, people who know how to use the Plan Ahead Method stand the best chance to get the most out of their lives.

Six Types of Plans

There are many types of plans and many types of time frames attached to this process. I have developed a system that uses six different types of planning. The six types of planning that I use closely parallel the five time periods that I use to categorize my goals. Here are my six types of plans:

1. Daily Plans. Daily plans are the most basic form of planning. Daily plans are critical to our success because they help us to connect "how" with "now." They join the future with today. Daily plans are full of detail and specific events and actions. This is where we must execute and act if we are to be successful and effective. Daily plans are the key to achieving our lifetime goals and objectives. I have learned that what I plan today determines what I will be able to accomplish today and tomorrow.

2. Weekly Plans. Weekly plans are the next most basic form of planning. As a teacher, I used this method to plan my instruction for many years. The small amount of time it takes to write out a weekly plan is a small investment that always pays big dividends in performance. I now use this type of planning method to write out my activities for each week of the year. Weekly plans provide an important link between our daily actions and our monthly goals.

3. Monthly Plans. Monthly plans provide the connection between our short and long-range targets. Monthly plans are not as detailed as daily or weekly plans. They are more likely to be partially completed outlines or works in progress. The important thing is that they help us anticipate actions, coordinate events, and schedule important activities. Monthly plans are important because they help us align our actions with our goals.

4. Quarterly and Semi-annual Plans. These types of plans form the foundation of the intermediate goal achievement process. The specific goals and priorities developed in these plans can help clarify day-to-day activities and link them to future actions, events, and projects. Quarterly and semi-annual plans provide important check-points that we can use to gauge our progress and make needed adjustments. They are written in general terms with very few specific times and dates.

5. One-Year and Two-year Plans. I learned the value of one and two-year plans in the military. These plans are fundamental to our long-range planning program. These plans are the links between our short-range plans and our lifetime plans. They focus on the near horizon and force you to think about many significant personal and professional choices that lie ahead. They help provide the long-term vision and motivation that is required to inspire the hard work and discipline that we need to work through the obstacles we encounter in our daily living.

6. Long-Range Plans. It pays to investigate the future, especially when it is yours! These types of plans focus on goals and objectives that go from three to fifty-years and beyond! In military and business circles these types of plans are called Strategic Plans. Long range plans are vague to begin with, but they are important for the vision they provide. These plans help us align our goals and objectives with our ultimate purpose for living. They provide a broad framework that outlines who we want to become and what contributions we want to make to the world. They can help us find the purpose for our work and our life. As we grow and learn and achieve some of our goals and objectives, we begin to develop a sharper focus. This sharper focus helps us add more and more details to the long-range plans as we go through life.

The Six Power Planning Questions

As we already learned, there are many kinds of plans. There are lesson plans, flight plans, game plans, campaign plans, battle plans, business plans, financial plans, and annual plans just to name a few. Each of these different planning methods has their own unique format and sequence. Every plan, no matter how simple or complex, must answer six basic questions. Those questions are: who, what, where, when, why, and how?

Whether you are planning a trip to the grocery store or a household move across the country, your planning process must answer the six basic questions. Although the size and complexity of these two projects are quite different, the process remains the same. To develop your How Power you must learn to ask the six power questions as you begin any new project or set any new goal. Learning to think in terms of these six questions is essential to effective planning and increased How Power. The answers to each of these questions will often lead to powerful results in your life. Now, it's time to take a close look at each of the six power questions.

1. "Who?" is the responsibility question. It determines the person or group that is accountable for the plan or certain parts of the plan. Ultimately, this is an important question because it identifies the person or team that will be responsible for achieving the desired results of the plan.

2. "What?" is the goal question. It establishes the results that will be achieved when the plan is executed to completion. "What" also describes the conditions that must be met to achieve the goal. This question should also identify the resources that will be required to execute the plan successfully. The better the answer, or answers, to the "what" question, the better the results.

The "what" question adds specificity to the plan. The more precise your goal, the more specific your plan should be. When more than one objective is desired in a plan, then priorities must be established. When planning you must always ask which objectives are most important and which one needs to be achieved first.

3. "Where?" is the location question. This important question identifies the place, or places, where the plan will be carried out. In a group setting, the steps in a plan may require the cooperation and assistance of many individuals from many different departments within an organization. Another plan may require the cooperative efforts of individuals and teams from different organizations. The "where" question is important because it helps to identify critical areas of coordination that must be achieved to ensure the ultimate success of the plan.

4. "When?" is the timing question. The "when" question helps establish the schedule for a plan's execution. The "when" question defines the beginning and the end of the plan. It should also describe the major phases of the project that will occur along the way. Asking "when" helps to ensure that the right things get done at the right time. Yes, each step in your plans should have a time/date target that can be used to measure progress.

5. "Why?" is the purpose question. This powerful question provides the reason, or reasons, that motivate the person or persons involved in the plan. This is an especially important question for individuals and groups. As one famous motivational phrase says, "You can do anything if you have enough 'whys." Finding your "why" is absolutely to getting the most out of your plans and your life!

6. "How?" is the process question. It establishes the process that will be used to accomplish the goal or objective of the plan. How is the question that defines the steps that need to be completed and the sequence for each step. This information is vital in the planning process because it helps break down large, complex procedures into manageable and measurable steps. A timeline also helps link all the questions by placing them in sequence so that the timing of the events can be identified. It helps determine priorities and allows you to get the most out of the time you have available to accomplish the task.

The Secrets of How Power

You should have a better understanding of the importance of How Power and what it can do for your life. Now, it is time to discover some planning secrets that have not been explored so far. The ideas in this section will elaborate on some of the concepts that have already been discussed and reveal many new insights about planning. These secrets are designed to help you become a power planner—a person who knows the value of planning and knows how to use it to bring out the best in himself and get the best out of life.

Secret #1
**Planning does not guarantee success,
but it certainly reduces the chances for failure.**

I am certain that you would agree that there are very few guarantees in life. Nobody can guarantee that every plan that you make will result in a huge success. However, I can guarantee that the plans you do not make are doomed to fail! It is often said that a dog is a man's best friend. I like dogs, but I truly believe that a man's best friend is a really good plan! People who take the time to plan have a great friend that can take them to success in every venture that they undertake.

Conversely, people who fail to plan increase the odds for failure and disappointment. One of my favorite expressions is, "A good beginning usually sets the stage for a good ending." Planning is always a good way to begin any undertaking, or effort. It is the ultimate tool that can help us set the stage for successful endings.

A good plan can help us turn our goals into reality. It can help us maximize our time and get the most out of all available resources. Plans allow us to think ahead and anticipate problems so that we can develop solutions in advance. Each question that we answer and each step that we take will bring us closer to our goal. Planning is a habit that we can develop and improve on as we grow and learn.

Secret #2

Goals provide the direction in life and plans provide the path.

In Chapter Three I stressed the important role that goals play in life. Goals have a critical place in the Choose and Grow Rich process because they bring focus to any life. Remember, the act of writing a goal on paper is the first step to making that goal a reality because it is now in a concrete form—words! Dr. Stephen R. Covey expressed it best when he said it "Begin with the end in mind." I would add, put that "end" or vision in writing.

Goals help us focus our efforts and energies like nothing else in life. They can give us the direction that we need to bring out the best in ourselves and our life. However, goals will create frustration and disappointment if they are not supported by effective plans and positive actions. A goal that is backed by a plan is a powerful force indeed. Plans are important because they serve as road maps that can guide our actions and take us to our goals. Plans help us create our best future. Having a destination is important, but planning helps us to select and navigate the right path.

Most of us are not foolish enough to begin a long trip without a map and directions to our destination. Yet, many people try to achieve personal success without goals and plans. I like to use the acronym MAP to discuss the importance of good planning. Think of a good plan as a Master Action Plan—a MAP that can take you from where you are to where you want to go. The best way to ensure that you get to where you want to go is to set a goal and develop a plan that will take you there.

Secret #3

It is always easier to revise a plan in the heat of battle than it is to create one.

The best time to write a plan is before you need it. The next best time is when you need it. The worst time to write a plan is after you need it. The important thing to remember is that any plan is better than no plan. A plan does not have to be perfect to be valuable. It does not even have to be completed to be useful. Plans should be considered a work in progress. If you can develop the habit of planning in advance, you will have an incredible advantage in dealing with any situation. The Israeli defense forces have a saying that sums it up best: "Every plan is the basis for change." I believe that changes to an existing plan are always easier than writing a new plan, especially when the pressure is on!

The most critical thing to remember about planning is that it is not an exact science. I have never encountered a perfect plan and I doubt that one has ever been written. Plans are not etched in stone. They can be modified along the way. They should be changed as your circumstances change. This is not a weakness in you or your plan; this is reality. As Publius Syrus said, "It is a bad plan that admits no modification."

Secret #4
Airline pilots cannot take off without a flight plan. Your life will not ever get off the ground without a life plan.

Living without a plan for your life is very risky business. We place our future success and prosperity at great risk when we undertake any project without a plan. Zig Ziglar called people who lack goals and plans, "wandering generalities." These people go through life one day at a time, but they do not have any specific goals or plans for what they really want to accomplish. Going through life without a plan is like shooting a rifle without aiming. It is like starting a journey without a map. We can get by with this approach, but goals and plans help us get there faster and easier.

People who don't have a plan for their life usually end up living the plan that everyone else has for them. Is this the way to really live your best life? Choosing to live without a plan automatically means that someone else will be in charge of your goals, your plans, and your life. These people can be your parents, your spouse, and even your boss. This does not mean that your life will be terrible, but it may not exactly be what you really want to do with your life.

Secret #5
Planning is a wise investment of time that always pays big dividends.

As I mentioned earlier in this chapter, many of my former students would tell me that they did not have time to plan or that planning was a waste of time. The driving question that we must all answer about how we invest our time is, "If you don't have time to do it right, when will you have time to do it over?" Yes, I acknowledge that planning is not always easy. I also admit that it takes time, valuable time, that many of us are too busy to invest.

However, that is precisely why planning is so important. If we believe that our goals are important and that our time is valuable, then planning becomes an incredibly wise investment of our precious time.

I learned one of my most powerful time and planning lessons during my third year of officer training in the U. S. Army Reserve Officer Training Corps. I was attending my advanced training field course where we were learning to perform basic soldier and leader skills with hundreds of students from across the Midwest. During a patrolling class, one of our instructors talked about the importance of reconnaissance and leadership planning. He told us that leaders had to learn the habit of doing as much reconnaissance as possible in the time allowed. Sometimes we would have sufficient time to seek out information about our mission and we may even have the luxury of conducting a leader reconnaissance and walk or drive to our objective and see it first-hand. However, in other situations we would only have enough time to study the map carefully before embarking on a mission. Regardless of how much time we had, he advised that we should get as much information as possible in the time allowed. Then he said, "No time spent in reconnaissance is ever wasted."

I have successfully applied my "planning" life lesson during many different situations in my life. Unfortunately, there have been some situations where I failed to invest the proper planning time up front and suffered the consequences later. Planning is a tool that we can use to increase our chances of getting things right the first time. I am a firm believer that planning is something that we must think of as an investment. I further believe that no time spent in planning is ever wasted. Learn to make wise investments of your time by planning and you will receive big dividends from this valuable process.

Secret #6
What you plan today determines what you will accomplish tomorrow.

I cannot estimate how many millions of people in the United States would not think of going to work in the morning without having a cup of coffee before they go out the door. Many of these people take their coffee with them as they drive, or ride, to work. If you ask them why their coffee is so important to them you get answers like:

- It gets me going in the morning.
- I cannot function in the morning without it.
- I really do not wake up until I have that first cup of coffee.

You get the picture, right? How many Americans leave for work in the morning without a plan for the day? I have a feeling that "many millions" is probably closest to reality. I am not a coffee drinker, but I understand how important coffee is to people. What is even more critical is how important plans are to successful living. Going out the door without a cup of coffee in the morning is the beginning of a bad day for millions of Americans. However, leaving home without a plan can really spell disaster!

Again, one of my favorite thoughts on planning is an anonymous quote that says, "A plan is a trap that is set to capture the future." I think everyone would like to trap their best life and live it to the fullest! The future that contains our dreams and hopes is certainly a desirable objective. Planning gives us the best chance to catch our desired future. How do you think Sir Edmund Hillary became the first man to climb Mount Everest? Do you think he had a plan, or did he just go for his daily walk and end up on top of the world's tallest mountain?

Plans do not just happen; we have to make them happen. I know that Edmund Hillary had a plan, a big plan. It could not have happened any other way. The goal was too big and the required resources were too great to approach this task without a plan. Sir Edmund Hillary invested the time and effort required to prepare for the arduous task of climbing a 29,000-foot mountain. He set a trap, he captured his best future. Of course, he did it one step at a time.

We can do the same. We can have our own Mount Everest and we can take the time to set the traps that will capture our dreams and goals. Sir Edmund Hillary took many "todays" to plan what he wanted to do tomorrow. He would tell you that it was necessary and that it was worth it, don't you think? Invest the time it takes to plan.

Secret #7
The power of a written plan is one of the most potent forces in the universe.

Again, I already wrote about the importance of written goals and how they sharpen our focus and energize our actions. Most people do not achieve their goals because they are not clearly defined. Plans, especially written plans, are critical to our achievements. Unfortunately, too many are afraid to plan because they believe that their plans have to be perfect. The good news is that plans do not have to be perfect, just sound. A sound plan is one that asks the six power questions (who, what, where, when, why and how) and puts the answers in writing!

The simple act of putting something in writing has a powerful effect on the subconscious mind. The process of writing a plan makes it a concrete entity to the subconscious mind. Instead of some abstract wish or dream, a written plan is something that the subconscious mind can comprehend and act on.

A written plan can be the perfect tool that will take you from where you are to where you want to be. Written plans act like a magnifying glass that focuses the sunlight on one specific spot. Such focused sunlight can start a fire almost instantly. Plans ignite the flame of enthusiasm and they keep the fire burning by organizing and sequencing our actions. Written plans help to ensure that we are making regular and consistent progress toward our goal. A well-written plan can keep you on the path to success and sustain your motivation. This kind of synergy creates a power that is difficult to explain, but it is a force that can help you bring out your best every day.

How to Increase Your How Power

Here are nine suggestions that you can use to increase your planning skills. These ideas will help you develop realistic, personalized plans that can successfully link your goals and dreams. You can use some, or all, of these techniques to become a power planner. Lasting success doesn't just happen. It happens one day, one plan, and one step at a time.

1. Ask the six power questions. Remember you do not need to be a perfect planner to succeed. However, you do need to be thorough. By using the six basic power questions consistently you will develop effective plans that will get any project off to a solid start. You should develop the habit of asking these questions for any task or goal that you want to achieve, no matter how big or how small. Learning to plan with these six questions in mind (who, what, where, when, why, and how) will help you become a more effective and a more powerful planner. That is the bottom line!

2. Use the power of brainstorming. Use the power of brainstorming to overcome the obstacles that you encounter during the development or execution of your plans. One technique you can use is a method called "Find Ten Ways." I learned this technique from the legendary television evangelist, Robert Schuller. When you encounter an obstacle in your plan, simply take out a sheet of paper and write down ten things that you can do to overcome the obstacle or turn it into an opportunity. They do not have to be logical, or even possible. Just start writing. You will be amazed at some of the powerful ideas you will discover with this simple process. Remember a big key to personal achievement lies in being "how" thinker. Use the Find Ten Ways method and become a powerful "how" thinker who excels at finding new ways to make your plans succeed.

3. Put your plans in writing. I know many people who do a lot of mental planning, but rarely put anything down on paper. While some people can make this system work, it is much more powerful to put your plans in writing. Written plans help us record, organize, and prioritize important tasks. All these benefits can improve our plans and increase their chances of success. The magical impact that written plans can have on our subconscious mind cannot be underestimated. I encourage you to use mental planning to develop your plans, but I strongly urge you to put them in writing. I believe that legendary personal development guru Jim Rohn, said it best: "Never begin the day until it is finished on paper."

4. Start small and build your skills. If you lack confidence in your ability to plan, you must start small and go slowly. Tackling too big a project in the beginning can result in setbacks that may dampen your enthusiasm and lead to discouragement.

The principle to follow is "keep it simple." Remember, we learned to crawl before we learned to walk. And we learned to walk before we learned to run. Take it one step at a time.

5. Make planning part of your daily routine. Develop the habit of planning by setting aside ten to fifteen minutes of planning time every day. This can become the most important and most productive time of your day. I strongly recommend that you schedule this time in the evening, about an hour before you go to bed. Look at your plans for the day, for tomorrow, and for the rest of the week. What do you need to do today, tomorrow, and this week to achieve some of your goals? Your plans should never collect dust. Instead, they should be tattered and worn at the edges. Review your plans frequently and update them as circumstances change.

6. Use planning tools to guide your efforts. I strongly recommend that you use some sort of a day planner or personal organizer that you keep with you throughout the day. There are many excellent systems available in a variety of price ranges. I find that the best ones are organized on a daily or weekly basis. These systems are invaluable in tracking your daily, weekly, and monthly progress towards executing your plans and the achieving your goals. In addition, I suggest that you use whatever systems or tools available in your industry or line of work. There are checklists, timelines, planning formats, and forms that you can use to develop the plans that you need to reach your personal and professional goals.

7. Energize your plans with action. Develop the habit of doing something every day to achieve at least one step toward a goal or goals. Make the phone call, send the letter, walk the mile, complete the report—just do something!

I am a great believer in planning. However, I am a bigger believer in action. Plans do not get things done; people do! Energize your plans with action and you can achieve anything that you want to accomplish. Put the power of planning to work in your life by energizing your plans with action. Pay attention to the words of General George S. Patton, Jr. who said, "A good plan violently executed now is better than a perfect plan next week." Yes, you are a living, breathing "action" machine. So, act like it!

8. Be flexible, be flexible, be flexible! Remember that there are no perfect plans. Also, remember that you do not ever want to create any perfect plans. The price that you pay for a perfect plan is always too high. Instead, develop good plans and start working on them quickly. You will improve them as you go along. You will discover what works and what does not work. You will learn new information that will cause you to develop different alternatives. Do not be threatened by this process. Understand it and use it to your advantage. Review your plans frequently, revise as necessary, take more action, and repeat until you succeed!

9. Plan your work then work your plan. Yes, we will finish this chapter the same way we started it. Planning is important. In fact, it is critical to our success. I hope that I have emphasized this point enough in this chapter. Unfortunately, planning your work is important, but it is not enough. Even your best plans will not work unless you do. Plans that are not backed with actions are not worth the paper they are written on.

Napoleon Hill believed that "desire" was the fuel that powered all significant achievements in life. I certainly don't disagree with his wisdom! Here is a simple formula that I developed to teach this concept:

Goals + Plans × Passionate Action = Success

We have come a long way in this book and we are getting close to the exciting conclusion! The last topic of this book is my favorite one. Now that you have reached this page, I am confident that you know how to "Plan your work." Now, it's time to find out how to "work" your plan.

CHAPTER 7

CHOOSE ACTION

Do it. Do it right. Do it right now.
—NASA Slogan

Yes, this NASA slogan is one of my all-time favorites. There is no confusion about the message here, is there? This is the kind of thinking that drives America's Space Program. It is also the mindset that can help you run your personal success program called "Life." This is an incredibly powerful way to live. Notice that the phrase does not say, "Do everything now" or "Do it all now." No, it just exhorts us to take the right action at the right time—as in NOW!

Writer Thomas Henry Huxley would probably agree with the NASA slogan since he said that "The great end in life is not knowledge but action." Knowledge is not power it is only the potential for power. The world's greatest ideas are worthless until they are put into action. Action, not knowledge, is true power and we should never confuse the two. We cannot build our best life entirely on what we know although knowledge can provide a good foundation.

Knowledge that is not used is of no more value than ignorance. We cannot build a life on what we are going to do. Life is made up of what happens, despite all our plans. If you want your life to turn out the way you want to, you must act, right? Yes, action is the primary tool that you must use to create the life that you desire.

I describe the ability to take action as Now Power. It is the final key to presenting the ideas that have been bringing dreams to life for centuries. Now Power is the habit of taking actions that yield desired results. It is the ability to get the right things done at the right time. Now Power is a "Do it Now" way of living that says, "I let my feet do the walking and my actions do the talking." If you genuinely want to achieve your goals and accomplish your plans, you will have to take action—lots of it. None of your goals are going to fall off a tree and hit you in the head. Huge sums of money are not going to drop into your lap or magically show up in your bank account.

If you want to increase your Now Power, you must learn how to energize you dreams, goals, and plans with action. You will have to speak with more verbs and live with more action. Wishing does not accomplish anything—only action does. Quite simply, Now Power is an understanding about life that says, "I don't wait for things to happen in my life, I make them happen!"

Why is Now Power So Important?

If you want your life to turn out the way you want it to, you must develop the habit of acting. Eventually, everything in life comes down to getting things done. You cannot build a good life on good intentions. The only way to build a good life is to take lots of good actions.

There are millions of people in the world who have big dreams, super ideas, and wonderful plans. However, the only ones who are living their dreams are the ones who acted on those dreams. Lots of talk and no action equals a life of failure and frustration.

One of my favorite quotes comes from talk show host Dr. Phil McGraw. He once stated that "Life rewards action." Action is the key to everything we have discussed so far in this book. Nothing happens unless someone makes it happen—somebody who takes action! You can believe everything that you have read so far, but if you do not take action, nothing will change. That is why the smallest action is always better than the greatest intention.

A famous life insurance executive, Mr. Albert E. N. Gray, authored an amazing publication titled *The Common Denominator of Success*. In that booklet, he bluntly stated that "Winners have simply formed the habit of doing things losers don't like to do."

(Gray, Page 5) One of the biggest differences between top achievers and people who come up short is action. The winners in life understand the power of action. They appreciate the fact that action is the primary tool that can help us be the best person that we can become. We have the power to master our own destiny. It all starts by acting. Any questions?

A Closer Look at Now Power

Did you know that the word "now" is actually the word "won" in reverse? If you look at the world's successful people, you will discover they have all won the game of life because of their actions. If you want to truly win the game of life, you need to do the same. Now Power is the habit of acting when it needs to be taken, not necessarily when you feel "inspired" to do it.

If you have formed the action habit it means that you are defeating many of the fears, doubts, attitudes, and other destructive habits that overcome millions of other people. It also means that you have probably won over procrastination more times than it has defeated you!

If you look back at your life and try to decide whether you are winning or losing, you will identify action as the magic ingredient that has made the most difference. If you feel that you are not where you want to be, you will probably remember lots of things that you wanted to do, intended to do, or planned to do, but just did not do. On the other hand, if you are happy with the progress you have made so far, you will be able to look back at the actions you took to get where you are now.

Most people do not regret doing too much in life, but they do regret doing too little, or not enough. The things that a person did not do are often remembered because of the pain they still cause. Dreams, goals, and plans that are not put into action can become great sources of frustration and regret.

Now Power is the only way to prevent this from happening in our life. The habit of action—the ability to get up and do something—is the key to your future success. The seeds of regret and disappointment are sown all over the fields of fear, doubt, and procrastination. The only way to keep from producing crops of disillusionment and despair is to get into action. Action is the key to Now Power. So, if Now Power is the key to living a life of personal and professional excellence, why don't more people take the actions necessary to ensure their success?

Why No Action?

There are lots of reasons why people do not take the action necessary to achieve their dreams and goals. My seminar students always heard about this topic in great depth in my classes on successful living. After many discussions, we always concluded that procrastination was the biggest reason for a lack of action in life.

Procrastination is basically the habit of putting off until tomorrow what could be accomplished today. We are all guilty of a little procrastination now and then, but when it becomes a consistent manner of behavior, we have a problem.

Procrastination is the father of the "F" twins—frustration and failure. If we do not understand this powerful enemy and take steps to defeat it, we will never be able to live our best life. There are hundreds of reasons why we fail to take the necessary actions that will allow us to be, know, feel, and do our best. Here are the top ten causes of procrastination that were identified by people like you in my seminar discussions:

1. Fear
2. Worry
3. Doubt
4. Task too difficult
5. Poor planning and poor use of time
6. Do not know where to start
7. Lack of focus
8. Lack of confidence
9. Not important enough
10. Perfectionitis

Do any of these reasons sound familiar?

I am sure that we have all stopped ourselves from acting by some of these reasons a few times in our life. Let us take a closer look at each one and discover their power that stops most people before they even start.

1. Fear. In my opinion, fear is Public Enemy Number One. There is an axiom that says, "Fear is the darkroom where negatives are developed." Fear probably holds back more people and prevents more progress than any single word in the universe. Fear, both real and imagined, is a vicious enemy that destroys millions of dreams, goals, and plans every day. Fear comes in many versions. There is fear of failure and fear of rejection. Believe it or not, fear of success and fear of inadequacy are also debilitating conditions.

2. Worry. Worry is right behind fear; it is definitely Public Enemy Number Two. If there was a way to calculate the cost of worry on productivity and personal success, it would be in the hundreds of billions of dollars. Excessive worry, or negative imagination as I call it, causes physical and mental problems that rob us of our confidence and self-assurance. Worry is a terrible misuse of our creative imagination and it consistently causes us to be less than our best. As Mary Engelbreit says, "Worrying does not empty tomorrow of its troubles. It empties today of its strength." Worry is not something we should take lightly. It is an enemy that we must defeat!

3. Doubt. Doubt is another crippling condition that holds us back and keeps us from acting in ways that will help us become the best that we can be. Doubt causes us to be uncertain and indecisive. It causes us to hesitate and wait when we should be taking action.

When we let doubt creep into our life we are definitely harboring an unwelcome and unfriendly guest. There is no doubt in my mind that you will never be able to live your best life until you defeat the doubts and doubters in your life!

4. Task too difficult. Yes, difficult tasks can make cowards of us all. A large project or challenge undertaking can be overwhelming, even for the most talented people. To attempt something that you have never done before can be terrifying. It causes us to be hesitant and ineffective. Big challenges will stop us in our tracks unless we develop strategies to overcome them. Amazing things can happen when you shift your thinking from how difficult something is to how you can break a problem down and defeat it with action!

5. Poor use of time. We have already discussed the issue of time in Chapter Five. Time can be our best friend or our worst enemy. When we consistently delay important actions, we begin to develop the habit of procrastination. Remember, I said that procrastination is "The habit of putting off until tomorrow what could be done today." Our inability to make good choices about our time can become a barrier that will stand between where we are and where we want to be.

6. Do not know where to start. If you have never accomplished something before, then you may not know where to start. You may lack knowledge or experience, or both. If you do not know where you are going, you will have difficulty getting there, right? The best way to handle a situation like this is to spend time learning as much as you can about the problem, or challenge, that you are trying to overcome. Then, develop a solid plan that has specific actions that need to be taken at each step along the way. Your plan will tell you where to start and it will provide a map that can help you get to your desired destination.

7. Lack of focus. A lack of focus is a serious problem for many people. Sometimes this affliction is disguised as laziness. However, it is often a symptom of a deeper problem caused by a lack of purpose and motivation. There are very few lazy people, but there are millions of people who really do not know why they are living on this earth. People who habitually fail to act are really saying, "I need a reason to get up out of my easy chair and get going." People who lack focus are usually missing the purpose and direction that all successful people possess. When somebody knows what they want in life and why they want it, they will find the desire to act.

8. Lack of confidence. I believe we are all born with confidence—lots of it. Think about it: babies could not learn to walk and talk without a huge amount of confidence. Unfortunately, many youngsters lose much of their innate confidence as they grow up. It then becomes a matter of how much confidence we can get back as we grow into adulthood. Yes, a lack of confidence is a form of fear that can develop into a big barrier between you and your success.

9. Not important or not rewarding. Many people fail to act because they see little or no value in the activity they are avoiding. This type of attitude is characterized by the "it's not worth it" philosophy. People who live without clarity and focus often fail to see the value in doing unpleasant tasks that could lead to greater accomplishments in the future. Yes, sometimes we need to do things that are hard and uncomfortable to get closer to something we really want. Many famous entertainers and business professionals worked their way through college by waiting tables, tending bars, and selling hamburgers. Everything we do has only as much meaning and value as we give it. We all have a choice in how we view everything we do. Unrewarding tasks will be exactly that if we fail to connect what we are doing now to what we want to be doing in the future.

10. Perfectionitis. Sadly, millions of people suffer from this terrible affliction. People who suffer from perfectionitis are less likely to act because they do not feel they can do it perfectly. The worst mistake we can make is to do nothing because we cannot do it exactly right. Perfection is almost impossible to achieve. When we stop ourselves from doing something because we cannot do it perfectly, we set ourselves up for a frustrating and unfulfilling life. The good news is that you do not have to be perfect to achieve success.

The Power of Action

One of the most powerful lessons I ever learned about action came from former Miss America and motivational speaker Marilyn Van Derbur. I heard her speak in Detroit, Michigan in 1976. Her inspiring presentation focused on three powerful words: **A**sk, **S**eek and **K**nock. Ms. Van Derbur spent her time talking about the powerful impact that these three words can have in life. Their important role in your personal success is further explained in the New American Bible, Matthew 7:7:

> **A**sk, and it will be given to you;
>
> **S**eek and you will find;
>
> **K**nock and the door will be opened to you.

The three keys are easy to remember when you think of the word ASK. Notice that all these words are verbs, not nouns. They are action words that require us to take a chance, to do something, to make things happen. Let us look at each one a little more closely.

Ask. Sometimes we must ask other people for help in order to achieve our goals. Maybe you need to schedule an appointment to talk with someone who has the knowledge, experience, or money that you will need to move forward on a project or goal.

Or maybe you need to make a phone call to ask for a job interview or a letter of recommendation. All of us need help to make our way in life. Asking is a powerful form of action that can get us the help we need to achieve our dreams and goals.

Seek. The word "seek" speaks to the essence of Now Power. The process of seeking requires us to go searching for the things we value most. Seeking is the act of personal discovery that we must all undertake if we are to be and do our best. The attempts that we make in the process give our life meaning and value. Our attempts to discover the life of our dreams gives us the knowledge and experience we need to achieve our destiny.

The only way to get where you want to go is to start taking one step at a time and keep on crawling, walking, or running until you get there. Ultimately, our best life does not come to us, we create it by seeking it out.

Knock. Knock represents a form of physical action that is difficult for most people to take. Have you ever had a job where you had to knock on doors and risk rejection with the opening of every door? I learned a great deal about myself, about other people, and about life all in one summer. My first job was in education. I was a teacher, which meant I had summers "off." Unfortunately, my pay stopped on the last day of school, but the bills kept coming in. So, I really did not have any summers off. I had to find work in the summer.

One summer, I sold encyclopedias door-to-door. I was twenty-four years old and it was pure torture in the beginning. I am right-handed, so my right hand was my door knocking hand. When I approached the house of a potential prospect my right hand seemed to weigh five hundred pounds! It was so difficult to do because I knew that every time I knocked on a door, I was setting myself up for rejection. Yes, and some rude treatment in some cases.

My sales manager, Jack Tod, knew how much trouble I was having. He taught me a simple lesson. He said that "You will fail to sell one-hundred percent of all the people you don't call on. If you want to sell encyclopedias you will have to knock on a lot of doors." All of us must knock on some unfriendly doors to be successful in life. We may not have to do door-to-door selling for a living, but there are other doors that we must approach and get open if we are to live our dreams and achieve our goals.

I believe that the best way to open the doors in your life is to knock, knock, and knock some more until you get it to open. History teaches us that **A**sking, **S**eeking, and **K**nocking are three important keys to increasing our ability to act. They are three powerful allies that will help you become the best person that you can be. Once you develop the habit of acting, you will develop the confidence that you need to accomplish more in your life. Ralph Waldo Emerson supported this concept when he said, "Do the thing and you will have the power." Now Power is within the reach of all of us if we will just take the time to ask when we need to ask, seek when we need to seek, and knock when we need to knock. You will be surprised at how many doors will open to you!

The Secrets of Now Power

Now, it's time to take a deeper look at Now Power. I have shared exactly seven secrets in each of the first six chapters of this book. However, I believe that Now Power is twice as important as any other topic in this book. So, I will share fourteen secrets in this chapter. These secrets will expand your understanding of this important concept and teach you more about how you can develop the habit of acting and accomplishing more of the things you want in your life. Get ready. This is going to be fun!

Secret #1
Ideas can inspire greatness, but only action can achieve it.

There are lots of people in this world who have great ideas and empty lives because they did not learn how, or when, to take action. One of the most powerful lines in the popular movie *Field of Dreams* came when Kevin Costner's character, Ray Kinsella, was talking about his father. Costner said, "He must have had dreams, but he never did anything about them." Ideas that are not connected to arms, legs, hands, and feet are destined to fail. We are living with false hope if we do not energize our dreams and aspirations with action.

Everything in this world is created in someone's imagination and that is where it will stay until it gets some action. The automobile, the telephone, and the Apple Computer are ideas that were acted upon by people like Henry Ford, Alexander Graham Bell, and Steve Jobs. Thoughts always precede action, but action gives life to our thoughts. All the world's great inventions were just ideas until someone took action and turned them into reality. Yes, action is the only thing that can bring life to our thoughts, dreams, and goals. That is why action is the key to greatness. Any questions?

Secret #2

Beginning is the first step to winning, but it is not the goal!

This simple truth is based on the Chinese proverb which says, "A journey of a thousand miles must begin with a single step." Every task, no matter how big or how small, must begin at some time and at some place. The first step is often the hardest, but it is the most important. The size of a task, big or small, can often keep us from taking that first step. We hesitate to begin a big task because it appears too overwhelming. Have you ever said to yourself, "It's just too big, I'll never be able to do it"?

William James wrote that "Nothing is as fatiguing as the eternal hanging of an uncompleted task." All of us have agonized over starting an important task. Yet, when we finally began the burdensome task, we often discovered that it was not as hard as we originally thought. The completion of any task, of any size, always provides a confidence boost. The size of a task is not important. What is important is getting started. Breaking a big task into smaller parts is one way to shrink an overwhelming job into something much more doable. The key to getting those easier tasks done is as simple as Nike's marketing mantra: Just do it! All tasks, big and small have a beginning. When you form the habit of acting, and then taking more action, you will be on the road to winning BIG in the game of life. As popular author Seth Godin says, "The important thing is always to start, but the objective is to finish."

Secret #3

You cannot spend your entire life aiming at targets, eventually you must pull the trigger.

Once again, action is the key to accomplishing what you want to achieve. We can dream all the dreams we want and we can even set goals to achieve them. We can develop detailed plans and visualize and affirm our impending success. However, if we do not put all of these ideas and techniques into action, it is all for nothing.

The only people who never fail are those who fail to try. Let's face it there are people who are afraid to pull the trigger for a variety of reasons. People who are afraid to pull the trigger in life are guaranteed one thing: failure. The baseball player who never swings the bat will never get a hit. The best he can hope for is a walk or to get hit by a pitch!

People who limit their thinking to settling for a walk in the game of life are shortchanging themselves. The real excitement is getting into the heat of the action and giving it your best effort. Yes, you may strike out or you may pull the trigger and miss the target, but you might hit a single or a home run! You could hit the target and even get a bullseye. As you know, life has few guarantees. However, I guarantee that you will fail to achieve every goal you set if you do not take action!

Secret #4
Doing something is always better than doing nothing.

Legendary college basketball coach John Wooden said, "Don't let what you cannot do interfere with what you can do." We may not be able to do everything, but we can all do something. Each of us can contribute in some way at some time. Even the smallest action gets you moving in the right direction. If you start poorly, that is good, at least you started. Besides, there are no prizes for starting, it is how you finish that counts.

There is an old English Proverb that says, "It is better to begin in the evening than not at all." Sometimes our days do not go as planned. We get involved in projects and activities that completely overwhelm us and take up an inordinate amount of our time. It is so easy to look at a day like this and say, "All is lost." At the end of a day like this you may feel that it is better to get some rest and start fresh in the morning.

However, a person with Now Power looks at it differently. He will look at the day's activities and figure out what went wrong and how it might be fixed the next day. She might take it even further by dwelling about how much of the day is left versus how much may have been lost to undesired activities or projects.

A person who has formed the action habit will decide that there is still time to do something. People with Now Power will overcome the temptation to make excuses. Instead, they continue to take a small action, or two, that will move them closer to achieving a goal or goals.

Secret #5
Greatness is rarely the result of one grand accomplishment. It is a series of smaller achievements that build and grow.

Who won the battle between the Colorado River and the flatlands in the western states? I believe it was the river, pursuing its course day in and day out for thousands of years. The steady flow of the water created a pattern of action that could not be stopped, and it shaped one of the great physical wonders of the universe—the Grand Canyon. This is the power of consistent, enthusiastic, and purposeful action.

How did Sir Edmund Hillary become the first man to climb Mount Everest, the tallest mountain in the world? He did it one step, one small step, at a time. Yes, the power of action—consistent, action can conquer the greatest obstacles. Success rarely comes in big chunks; instead, it manifests itself in small steps that lead to bigger steps and eventually large strides. Just like the snowball that rolls downhill, action starts small and slow and builds crushing power and momentum.

Secret #6
What you think determines your outlook on life. What you do determines your destiny.

Action is really what determines our bottom line in life. We can have great thoughts, great dreams, and great goals; however, if we do not put some action into them, we will end up with more frustration and less satisfaction.

Remember, the shortest distance between our dreams and our achievements is action. Our thoughts determine what we want in life, but our actions determine what we get. We have the power to control so much more than we think is possible. The primary tool for exerting the maximum amount of control is action. We all have the power to initiate as much action as we want to in our life. There is no set limit on the amount of action we can take. It is always our choice. Action is our greatest ally in the journey to be and do our best. The greatest truth about Now Power is that tomorrow's success depends on today's action.

Secret #7
The biggest difference between people who want and people who have is action.

Intelligence is often thought to be a great discriminator in life, but there are lots of bright people in the world who fall short of achieving their potential. Other discriminators such as age, race, religion, and sex are often thought to be the biggest determinants of personal and professional success. However, the facts tell us a different story. There are successful people from all walks of life who are not burdened by discrimination in their lives. They faced barriers because of their age, race, religion, or sex and they succeeded despite the problems they encountered. The primary tool that they used to overcome their problems was action.

There are basically two kinds of people. There are those who formed the habit of acting and there are those who formed the habit of making excuses. I know this is a broad generalization. But think about it. How many successful people do you know who are lazy? I do not know any and I seriously doubt that there are too many living on this earth.

People who know how to act are capable of producing a variety of successful outcomes in their lives. In contrast, think about people who I call "excuse machines." They are the ones who always have an excuse for why they failed to graduate from college, why their marriage failed, and why their new job did not work out. People who develop the habit of creating excuses instead of creating desired results are destined to excuse themselves into a frustrating and unfulfilling life.

It does not have to be this way. Action is the difference maker. The habit of acting instead of making excuses is one of the most powerful forces in the world. Remember, action is the primary force that can drive you towards your dreams and goals. It is the key to living the best life of all—a life of choice.

Secret #8
Your words are vital tools for increasing your ability to take action when you need to take it.

Yes, your words are vital tools that can help you increase your Now Power and put more action in your life. In Chapter Four we learned about the importance of Say Power and how to make our words work for us instead of against us. Your words should be your greatest ally, not your greatest enemy. The way we talk to ourselves has a tremendous impact on what we think, say, and do. We must use our words to build the mental and physical habits that will energize us and cause us to act when necessary. Now Power teaches us that life is a noun and live is a verb. If we want to truly live our best life, we must get into action.

W. Clement Stone popularized a simple phrase that has been used by millions of people to motivate themselves to action. The three words "Do It Now" have been powerful action activators for nearly fifty years.

The Nike Corporation developed a three-word advertising slogan that helped shape fitness attitudes for nearly thirty years. "Just Do It" became the mantra for the fitness revolution in the United States. Millions of people around the world took to the streets in their Nike shoes and running clothes. Imagine how much action and how much sweat these three words caused over the years. Of course, the NASA mantra that I introduced at the beginning of this chapter is my favorite.

Do you think these words have had any part in the success of the space program? I think they do because of the simple, powerful message that they communicate. Your words can be one of the most valuable tools that you can ever use to take the actions necessary to achieve your personal and professional goals.

Secret #9

The more you do, the more you will be able to do.

American businesswoman Rosabeth Moss Kanter says that "Power is the ability to get things done." I am sure that she would agree with the saying, "Actions speak louder than words." I agree with her concept because things like wishes, dreams, goals, and ideas are merely the *potential* for power. Action is the only way to get things done; it is the greatest source of our personal power. The beauty of action is that it grows confidence. During the writing of this chapter, I had the privilege of watching my first granddaughter learn to walk. Erin would take one step and down she would go, but she kept on trying and soon she was able to take two steps, and then three and four. The more action she took, the more she was able to accomplish. Action grows confidence and the more confident you become, the more action you are likely to take. You cannot learn to walk by reading about it or thinking about it, you just have to do it.

I learned these same lessons when I was training for my first marathon. The longest distance I had ever completed prior to setting this ambitious goal was six miles. How was I going to learn to run the twenty-six-mile race when I was so inexperienced and out of shape? I did some research and found a training plan suggested by Bill Rogers, one of the most successful marathoners in American running history. His training program was designed to condition the body gradually with steady increases in weekly mileage.

My confidence grew each week as I began to complete eight, nine, and ten-mile training runs. Eventually, I completed a twenty-two-mile run just two weeks before the race. Because of my training, I was confident and ready on race day. I took consistent, gradual action for over three months and achieved my goal of completing my first marathon.

Secret #10

Now Power is simply the habit of getting the right things done at the right time.

There is an adage that says, "Timing is everything." Sometimes we must get certain things done at certain times if we are to be successful and achieve a goal. Some actions can be delayed, but if we wait too long, it may be too late. One of the keys to Now Power is the ability to determine the real priorities in your life. There always seems to be more things to do than there is time to do them. We have already discussed the importance of putting first things first in our lives and getting the most out of every hour and every day.

Remember, one of the best ways to consistently get the right things done at the right time is to use the WIN question technique that I explained in Chapter Five. This simple technique will help you "win" the day—every day! Form the habit of asking, "What's Important Now?"

This simple habit can keep you focused on your goals and can lead to the kind of action that will help you get the right things done at the right time. Try it—it really works!

Secret #11

If you wait for the perfect time to begin a project you will probably wait forever.

There is never a perfect time to do anything. No matter how much planning you do, something will happen that you did not plan for. Hopefully, it will be something minor and you will be able to adjust without too much difficulty. In June 1944 Army General Dwight Eisenhower had to make one of the most difficult decisions in history of the world. He oversaw Operation Overlord, the Allied invasion of Normandy, which was the first phase of a comprehensive plan to defeat Hitler and free Europe from Nazi control. The survival of the free world was at stake and the entire operation was in danger of being postponed because of bad weather. A delay could jeopardize the entire mission because of the large size of the invading force and the difficulty of protecting its secrecy from German intelligence forces.

When General Eisenhower made his decision to start the invasion, he was accepting a sizeable amount of risk. The element of surprise would be lost if he delayed for any length of time. General Eisenhower knew that he could not wait for the perfect time. Whatever problems the weather posed would also affect the German forces. Ultimately, he acted and launched the greatest invasion in the history of modern warfare. I often wonder what might have happened if General Eisenhower had been more cautious and delayed his decision in hopes of better weather conditions. Yes, it was a world changing decision!

People who know the secrets of Now Power know that there is a time for waiting and a time for action. In most situations, action is the key to success and delays often result in missed opportunities and even failure. Develop the habit of acting when the situation warrants and be prepared to be flexible along the way. Dr. Samuel Johnson had a great quote about this topic. He said that "Nothing will ever be attempted if all possible objections must first be overcome." You do not have to make a perfect decision before you take action; decide what needs to be done, do it, and keep taking action until you achieve your goal.

Secret #12
Sometimes you will not feel like taking action, take action anyway!

Sometimes you will not feel like taking action, take action anyway! Okay, the point I am trying to make is we need to form the habit of doing things that failures do not like to do. If action is the habit that will take us to our goals, we need to forge this habit into our personality. It needs to become a part of who we are. Ultimately, you must form the habit of acting, lots of action to live your dreams and achieve the goals that you have set for yourself. Fatigue, bad moods, sadness, stress, shyness, and laziness are the arch enemies of action. Any excuse that you allow to deter you becomes another obstacle between you and your goals.

Jerry West, a college and professional hall of fame basketball player, expressed it best when he said, "You can't get much done in life if you only work on the days when you feel good." Yes, there are plenty of reasons to put off until tomorrow what needs to be done today. "I am too tired" and "I do not feel like doing anything right now" are both real show-stoppers.

Unfortunately, the problem is that excuses are stopping your show! It is impossible not to feel fatigue, sadness, and lethargy, but we do not have to give in to these feelings and emotions. Learning to recognize what is going on and acting anyway is a habit that will put you in position to get things done, even when you are not at your best. This kind of discipline will also put you in position to get great things done when you are feeling better. We cannot always be at our best, but we can always take some small action that will get us closer to our goals. Remember, it is okay to feel like not taking action. When this happens, find the power to do it anyway!

Secret #13
Beware of the "Busy Trap."

The "Busy Trap" is a place that we all fall into at one time or another. Rearranging your desk is a necessary task sometimes, but a messy desk will not keep you from achieving your dreams. Spending endless hours on Social Media probably won't help you achieve your most important goals. The key is to realize that being busy is rarely enough to get us where we want to go. Henry David Thoreau expressed this concept perfectly when he said, "It's not enough to be busy. The question is, "What are we busy about?"

Action is an act of will that we take for a specific reason. Action is focused, it is intentional, and it demands results! Walking around in a circle will keep you busy, but if you are trying to get from point A to point B the circle route probably will not get you there. The more times you act in a way that will get you one step closer to an important goal, the better your life will be. Strive to be a person who takes the right action at the right time. Life is not about being busy. Instead of falling into the "Busy Trap" be a person who is focused on taking action and getting the right things done at the right time.

Secret #14
Sometimes the best choice is to rest and re-charge.

Please understand that Now Power is not about being so focused and motivated to take action that you neglect your health and your loved ones. The primary goal of the Life Power philosophy is to help you build a life of balance and consistency that reduces the negative stress in your life.

Action is the only way to get things done! I think I have made my point about that concept. Yet, the best action to take in some instances is to do nothing or almost nothing. If you need to take a break then take a break. If you need to get some extra rest, then that is the best action you can take at the time, especially if you are sick. The same goes for recreation, exercise, hobbies, and other activities that are meaningful and important in your life. If you are so driven to achieve results and take action that you cannot relax or enjoy your family, you are headed for a big crash. It is not just okay to take a break, chill out, relax, and have fun—it is necessary. Taking time to re-charge your batteries and re-connect with your spouse, children, or loved ones is one of the best things you can do to maximize your time and live your best life.

How to Increase Your Now Power

Here are ten actions that you can take to increase your Now Power and decrease the delays and procrastination in your life. These ideas can help you take more action and create the habit of action in your life. Remember, the word "now" is the word "won" in reverse. Every time you act it means you have won over the fears and doubts that stop most people in their tracks. Use these techniques to help bring out the best in yourself and create the life of your dreams.

1. ASK More. Remember the three key words to creating the action habit: **A**sk, **S**eek, and **K**nock. If you want more action in your life you will have to take more action, risk more failure, and expect to be disappointed more often than the person who does not take action. You can also expect to achieve more, experience more success, and live with greater satisfaction. The rewards of action are worth all the risks—all you must do is ASK!

2. Confront procrastination. Examine your procrastination patterns and overcome them with action. Yes, everyone puts things off from time to time. However, if procrastination is a consistent part of your behavior, then it is a problem that you must deal with. Determine the situations where you are most likely to delay action and develop positive strategies to act when and where you need to. Delay can be a good strategy, but constant procrastination is a path to failure and frustration. Learning to overcome procrastination is something that you must do to maximize your Now Power. Any questions?

3. Be a starter and a finisher. Yes, a journey of a thousand miles does begin with the first step. However, if one step is all you take, you will never get where you want to go. One step is enough to get you started, but it will not enable you to finish too many projects. Starting is important, but finishing is the best way to ensure your success. Learn to take action, repeated action, until you get to where you want to be. I have a saying that says, "Your own successes you will rob, unless you learn to finish the job." People who are finishers learn to gets things done. Take time to update your "Life List" frequently. This is a great way to track your progress and document your success. Remember, the first step is always important, but finishing the journey is the goal!

4. Break big goals and projects into smaller parts. There is magic in thinking big, but when it is time for action big can be very intimidating. You may have heard the saying, "The best way to eat an elephant is one bite at a time." This is good advice for lots of things, not just elephant eating. Even the most challenging goal can be broken down into smaller steps that do not appear to be so intimidating. Always remember to take one step at a time and you can achieve any goal you set!

5. Use the power of one. You do not have to do everything in one day. Once you break your goal or project into smaller parts, take it one step at a time. Make a point to accomplish at least one thing every day that will get you closer to achieving an important goal. Action always results in some sort of progress. This the method that created the Grand Canyon and it can help you create a grand life! Take your dreams, your goals, and your life, one day, one step, and one action at a time.

6. Use more power phrases in your sentences. Your words have a tremendous impact on your habits and your ability to act. Words are powerful tools that we can use to build patterns of thought and action. Make a conscious effort to incorporate more power phrases in your sentences and you will send powerful messages to your subconscious mind about the person you are and will continue to become. Instead of saying things like "I'm really lazy" affirm that "I'm full of energy and enthusiasm today." Use affirmations and action activators to program yourself for action. One of the best things you can do for yourself is use the power of words to program your thoughts. Say to yourself, "I am a person who makes things happen" or "I take action and I know how to get thing done." Use action activators like the ones listed below to help you develop the habit of Now Power:

- Just do it
- Do it now
- I will do it. I will do it right. I will do it right now.
- I will start now

7. Use action to get action. Too many people approach action the way that famous baseball player, Satchel Paige, used to approach exercise. Satchel used to say, "When I feel the urge to exercise, I just sit back and relax until the feeling goes away." Too many people are waiting for something outside themselves to cause them to act. If you get in the habit of waiting for something to move you— may wait forever! If you want action, you will have to use the power of your own dreams, goals, and plans, to move yourself! Action begets action. The only way to give life to your ideas is to energize them with motion and emotion.

8. Face your fears and immobilize them with action. Always remember that fear is really an acronym for "**F**alse **E**vidence **A**ppearing **R**eal." Action is the enemy of fear. Fear is no match for determined actions that are powered by a belief in a worthy purpose. Ralph Waldo Emerson advised us to "Do the thing you fear and the death of fear is certain." Worry will not defeat fear and procrastination will not either. Instead, they feed our fears and give them the power to stop us and kill our dreams. Action is the only way to crush the fears that immobilize us and prevent us from being and doing our best.

9. Schedule power sessions and take a lot of action. I learned this valuable technique from an article about writer's block. The idea behind it is simple. If you are having trouble getting started on a project, schedule five or ten minutes to work on the project. Go to where you need to be to complete the project and have whatever tools or equipment you need to accomplish the task.

Set a timer or alarm for the allotted time and then get to work! Work as hard as you can to write, paint, saw, hammer, or talk for the entire time you set for yourself. At the end of the allotted time, you can determine whether you want to continue with the activity or not, but you will have made significant progress for two reasons. First, you got started and second, you have less to do the next time you work on the task.

10. Ask the WIN question frequently! Okay, I promise that this is the last time you will hear about the WIN question. If you want to consistently get the most out of your time and your life, you must be asking the WIN question frequently each day. This simple question will help you maximize your time by ensuring that you are always aware of your priorities and focused on what actions need to be accomplished. The more you ask the WIN question, the better your life will be.

Here is another thought to consider. Listed below is a billboard sign that was on I-294 heading south on I-294 near O'Hare Airport in Chicago. I first saw this sign in January 2006 and I really liked it. It is a slightly different take on the famous quote, "I think, therefore I am." by French philosopher René Descartes.

Ultimately, life comes down to what we do. We can say we are going to do something, promise that we will do something and hope that we will do something with our lives. However, none of these Said, "Life is the sum of our choices." concepts accomplish anything. If time is the great equalizer, then, action is the divider.

> **I do, therefore I am.**
> **Nextel Phones**

There are thousands of people who like to make promises about what they intend to do. Others tell everyone what they are going to do, but just cannot seem to get anything done. Ultimately, action is the only thing that builds loyalty and trust. It truly does separate the pretenders and the contenders. Andrew Carnegie put it all in perspective when he said, "As I grow older, I pay less attention to what men say. I just watch what they do."

I hope you act on all the topics of this book—there are seventy-five specific things to do, in case you were not counting. However, if all you do is make better choices, think positively, set goals, watch your words, and plan to use your time wisely, I will have failed in my efforts to teach and motivate you to live your best life. The key to living a life of your dreams with an abundance of wealth, success and lasting relationships all comes down to action. The only way to get where you want to go is by acting—day in and day out for the rest of your life!

Yes, everything in this book counts, but action counts more! In fact, maybe ten times more. Remember you are a living, breathing walking, talking, action machine. So, start acting like one!

Now, I want you to think about the final quote in this book.

**There are two primary choices in life;
to accept conditions as they exist
or accept the responsibility for changing them.
Denis Waitley**

What is your choice?

Better health?
More wealth?
Better relationships?
More career success?
Why not Choose to have it all?

BIBLIOGRAPHY

Addington, Jack. *Psychogenisis: Everything Begins in Mind.* New York: Dodd and Mead and Company, 1971.

Bristol, Claude M. *The Magic of Believing.* Garden City, New York: Ixia press, 2019.

Covey, Stephen R. *The 7 Habits of Highly Effective People.* New York: Simon and Schuster, 1989.

Gray, Albert. *The Common Denominator of Success.* Washington, DC: The National Association of Life Underwriters, 1976.

Hardy, Darren. *Success: Quotes for Achievers.* Plano, TX: Success Books, 2008.

Helmstetter, Shad. *What to Say When You Talk to Yourself.* New York: Gallery Books, 1986.

Hill, Napoleon. *Think and Grow Rich.* Los Angeles: Renaissance Books, 1960.

Hill, Napoleon. *The 5 Essential Principles of Think and Grow Rich.* Simple Truths: Naperville, IL. 2018.

Kohe, J. Martin. *Your Greatest Power.* Chicago: Success Unlimited, Incorporated, 1953.

Mackenzie, Alec. *The Time Trap.* New York: Amacom Books, 1990.

Maltz, Maxwell. *Psycho-Cybernetics.* New York: Pocket Books, 1960.

McGuinnes, Alan Loy. *The Power of Optimism.* San Francisco: Harper and Row, 1990.

Murphy, Joseph. Revised by Ian McMahon. *The Power of Your Subconscious Mind*. Paramus: Reward Books, 2000.

Peale, Norman Vincent. *The Power of Positive Thinking*. New York: Ballantine Books, 1956.

Potter, Alice. *The Positive Thinker: Self-Motivating Strategies for Personal Success*. New York: Berkley Publishing Group, 1994.

Schuller, Robert. *Tough Times Never Last, But Tough People Do*. Nashville: Thomas Nelson Publishers, 1983.

Seligman, Martin. *Learned Optimism: How to Change Your Mind and Your Life*. New York: Pocket Books, 1998.

Stone, W. Clement. *Success Through a Positive Mental Attitude*. New York: Pocket Books, 1960.

Sullivan Gordon R. and Michael V. Harper. *Hope is Not A Method: What Business Leaders Can Learn from America's Army*. New York: Random House (Times Books), 1996.

Webster, Merriam. *Webster's Collegiate Dictionary Tenth Edition*. Springfield, MA: Merriam-Webster, Incorporated, 2001.

Ziglar, Zig. *See You at the Top*. Gretna: Pelican Publishing, 1977.

ACKNOWLEDGEMENTS

Writing a book is mostly a lonely journey that can take months and years to complete. Yes, you just must spend a lot of time in isolation with your notes, your thoughts, and your computer. Fortunately, the journey is always easier when you have the love and support of family and friends.

First, I have to thank my loving wife, Carol, for her love and support. She is my #1 fan, and I am so fortunate to share my life with her. I am also grateful for the technical support of my son-in-law Richard Peel which saved me a lot of time in the preparation of the final version of this book.

Second, I am grateful to my high school English teacher, Mr. Richard Hill. He taught me how to write and created a passion for writing that I carry with me today. It is amazing how one exceptional teacher can positively impact an immature, lazy young man for the rest of his life!

Third, I am thankful for the many positive role models that I have met and studied over the years. The first "self-help" book that I ever read was *The Greatest Salesman in the World* by Og Mandino. Then I read *The Power of Positive Thinking* by Dr. Norman Vincent Peale and *The Positive Thinker* by Alice Potter. Of course, *Think and Grow Rich* by Napoleon Hill also had a great impact on my life as did *Your Greatest Power* by J. Martin Kohe. I was a college graduate, but I had never read books like this in high school or college. Now, I have read over 100 of these motivational, self-development books. I have been fortunate to meet giants in the field like Dr. Peale, Jesse Owens, Bob Richards, Marilyn Van Derbur, and John Wooden. The impact that these great Americans have had on my life has been significant! I owe an eternal debt of gratitude to all the authors who have helped me improve my life!

Fourth, I had the privilege of working with Dr. Thomas Bleet in the early 1980s. We were the first high school in the State of Michigan to develop a course in positive thinking, goals setting and other important life skills. I was fortunate to teach this pioneering course to high school students and adults for four of the most exciting years of my life! Unfortunately, this amazing course was not part of the "basic" curriculum and when a recession forced some budget cuts, the course ended. Of course, that was one of the most disappointing events of my life and it caused me to leave public education in 1983. Now, I focus my energy on new ways to deliver my thoughts on choices, Power Thinking, Hour Power, and many other important topics that help people live their best lives.

Finally, I genuinely appreciate the great work by my book design team at eBooks2go. Leslie Chirchirillo and John Bean are delightful to work with and so professional. Truly a dynamic publishing duo in my book. Thanks Leslie and John for all the great work you did to bring this book to life.

ABOUT THE AUTHOR

Photo Courtesy of Mike Tanner, Saint Mike's Photography

Barry Gallagher is a former Army officer, teacher, coach, and school administrator. He served successfully in a variety of leadership positions for over forty years. Gallagher has been writing, teaching, and speaking about the power of choice since 1976.

If you enjoyed this book, it would be great if you could leave a positive review on Amazon. It is quite easy to do and I would really appreciate it. Thank You!

For quantity purchase discounts contact Barry Gallagher:

E-Mail: PowerGroup@comcast.net

Other Books by Barry Gallagher:

- *Teacher STRONG-Daily Quotes to Inspire America's Teachers*
- *Leader STRONG: Daily Quotes to Inspire Leaders Everywhere*
- *The Nasty Football History of Michigan vs Michigan State*
- *Michigan Football's Greatest Era*
- *The Secrets of Life Power*
- *How to Get a Kick Out of Coaching Youth Soccer*
- *The Nasty Football History of Michigan and Michigan State – 1898 to 2021*
- *The Greatest Football Story Ever Told: Michigan vs. Ohio State – 1897 to 2022*